# FAMIL.
# *BUSINESS*
# MANAGEMENT

Dr. Andreas Svoboda

## Disclaimer

This eBook is for informational purposes only. The author is not an expert in the fields discussed and the information presented should not be considered as professional advice. Use the information in this eBook at your own risk.

I tried to make sure the info is accurate, but we can't promise it is perfect. I am not responsible for any errors or results that come from using this information.

***You can't copy or share this eBook without the author's permission.***

# CONTENTS

# INTRODUCTION

Many economies, both established and emerging, rely on family companies to forge a combination of family values, traditions, and commercial savvy. These businesses, which arose from the fusion of family relationships and commerce, play a critical role in creating jobs, spurring innovation, and contributing significantly to global GDP. They do, however, function with their own set of complexities coming from the confluence of professional and personal worlds. "Family Business Management" goes into the heart of these enterprises, uncovering their unique dynamics and providing insights into successful management.

We begin by defining a family company and focusing light on its ubiquity across several sectors. This sets the tone for understanding the particular traits that identify these businesses and the difficulties they often face. While the foundation is founded on trust, shared history, and ideals, maintaining a family company is not without challenges.

In terms of ownership and governance, our first chapter looks at the various ownership forms used by family companies. We investigate governance arrangements, examining their significant influence on the firm and its stakeholders. A critical issue here is the ability to balance family interests with the realistic objectives of the company while ensuring that neither is jeopardized.

The focus of our second chapter is succession planning, which is a characteristic of family company longevity. We emphasize its importance while also outlining ways for identifying and developing next-generation leaders. The complexities of educating both family and non-family individuals for leadership positions are also discussed, highlighting the differences that distinguish family enterprises.

The third chapter focuses on conflict, which is typically present when professional and personal domains collide. Here, we unravel the complexities of disagreements, providing insightful conflict resolution advice. Effective communication is examined in depth, with tactics for achieving agreement during decision-making outlined.

Our fourth chapter, Financial Management, debunks the financial foundations critical to the long-term viability of family businesses. This part covers the fiscal foundations that support these businesses, from budgeting methods to precise financial planning and from analyzing financing choices to managing intergenerational wealth.

We now shift our focus to human resources in the fifth chapter. Aside from the usual recruiting and personnel management issues, family firms provide a rich tapestry of complexity. We examine recruiting procedures and criteria, as well as how to create a positive working atmosphere.

Recognizing the imperatives of adaptability, corporate development, and innovation, chapter six delves into diversification and expansion plans. As markets change, so must family companies, and this part focuses on ways to maintain competitiveness and innovation.

Exiting a family company, whether by choice or by necessity, is fraught with complications. Chapter seven walks readers through several departure possibilities, the complexities of selling a firm, and planning for a smooth generational transfer.

The focus of our eighth chapter is legal and tax complexities, which are critical but frequently perplexing. Here, we examine the specific legal issues that family companies confront, as well as ways to reduce tax obligations and ensure compliance with a tangle of rules.

Our ninth chapter is grounded in reality, offering readers with case studies of successful family companies. These tales, rich with insights and lessons, serve as a mirror to the theory, enabling readers to correlate and understand.

The tenth chapter focuses on ethics and social responsibility, which are the foundations of many family enterprises. In delving into the ethical quandaries, we highlight the critical role that these businesses play in their communities and the greater social framework.

Our eleventh chapter focuses on managing family interactions, which are often at the core of these businesses. We explore the personal components that often interact with professional issues, from the impact of these interactions on decision-making to establishing trust and defining limits.

Our eleventh chapter takes a global view. We evaluate and analyze how cultural variables impact family company management across continents, offering a complete knowledge of family firms from a global perspective.

CHAPTER 1

# OWNERSHIP AND GOVERNANCE

Ownership and governance are two fundamental pillars of family business management that work together to guarantee a company's longevity and success. They are significant for a variety of reasons, impacting the enterprise's relationships with both internal and external stakeholders.

Ownership in a family business entails more than just financial investments; it also entails a strong emotional and historical attachment to the company. This close connection often indicates that the owners are really involved in the company's well-being and long-term success. Decisions are often assessed through the prism of both corporate acumen and family heritage. Owners are motivated by intrinsic incentives to favor long-term growth above short-term benefits.

However, this close bond may also be a source of difficulty. Conflicts may arise when emotions and business choices collide. This is where governance comes into play. Governance structures and procedures serve as a guiding framework for corporate operations, ensuring that they remain objective, professional, and consistent with the company's long-term objectives. It acts as a link between the emotional aspects of ownership and the pragmatic requirements of operating a firm.

In most family companies, good governance includes clearly defined roles and duties, decision-making procedures, and conflict-resolution systems. It guarantees that the family's values and company objectives are kept while simultaneously adjusting to changing business conditions and market dynamics.

Governance is also essential for succession planning. Transitioning from one generation to the next is one of the most difficult stages of any family company. This shift may become a chaotic moment without defined governance mechanisms, affecting the fundamental fabric of the firm. Effective governance clarifies leadership responsibilities, decision rights, and the company's future direction, resulting in a smoother generational transition.

Governance also develops trust among family members and other stakeholders. When responsibilities are clearly defined, and transparent procedures are in place, ambiguities and possible conflicts are reduced. Employees, customers, and investors are more inclined to trust a well-governed family firm because they know it is not affected by human whims but runs according to established norms.

While ownership provides a family firm with its own identity and intrinsic purpose, governance equips it with the skills and frameworks necessary to negotiate the challenges of both the familial and corporate worlds. The interaction of these two factors is critical in ensuring that a family company stays resilient, adaptable, and thrives over generations.

## Different ownership models in family businesses

### The Evolution of Ownership Models Over Generations

As ownership patterns pass from one generation to the next, family companies have undergone a remarkable development. This transition is inextricably linked to the increasing complexities of corporate operations, family relationships, and external market variables.

In their early phases, family firms are often formed as sole proprietorships, with a single person, the founder, exercising complete ownership and management. This paradigm is simple and easy to implement. However, it lacks depth in resources and viewpoints. The ownership model tends to alter as the firm expands and additional family members get engaged to suit their responsibilities and stakes in the company.

Partnership or joint ownership structures are often used by the second generation. Siblings or close relatives share ownership in this case, either equally or depending on their engagement or investment. While this model capitalizes on family members' joint abilities and resources, it also presents complications in decision-making, profit-sharing, and dispute resolution.

As the family tree grows to the third generation and beyond, the ownership paradigm becomes increasingly fractured. This might result in the formation of family consortia or holding businesses. Such arrangements seek to distinguish between family members who actively participate in company operations and those who are essentially passive investors.

However, when the ownership pool grows, there is a danger of diminished control and vision. To maintain coherence in corporate direction, protect family values, and handle possible conflicts, governance structures such as family councils or boards must be established.

The development of ownership patterns demonstrates the flexibility and resilience of family companies. It demonstrates their capacity to reconcile retaining ancestral heritage with adjusting to new business environments.

### The Interplay Between Ownership and Corporate Governance

The link between family company ownership types and corporate governance is dynamic, with one strongly impacting the other. Corporate governance, or the structures, procedures, and principles that govern a corporation, is critical to ensuring that the organization functions successfully, transparently, and in the best interests of all stakeholders.

A good corporate governance framework is needed in family enterprises because ownership may be distributed among different family members to preserve clarity of direction, accountability, and authority. The board of directors, for example, may contribute varied viewpoints, knowledge, and impartiality, ensuring that company decisions are not overly swayed by personal ties or emotions.

Furthermore, as the company expands and diversifies, the management complexities increase. Clear governance frameworks aid in delineating family members' duties and establishing boundaries between family matters and corporate concerns. This not only promotes easier operations but also reduces the likelihood of disputes caused by overlapping personal and professional realms.

Another critical component is the protection of minority interests. There is a danger that strong family factions may eclipse the interests of minority owners in family enterprises with diverse ownership positions. Robust corporate governance processes guarantee that all stakeholders' rights, regardless of ownership size, are respected and that they have a voice in critical company decisions (Governing the Family-Run Business, 2001).

The ownership model in family companies is about orchestrating a harmonic balance of family tradition and current governance methods, not only share distribution. Family companies may pave the road for sustainable development, enduring legacies, and happy family connections by recognizing and resolving the symbiotic link between ownership and corporate governance.

## The Role of Family Councils in Ensuring Cohesion

Family councils have arisen as important governance structures, particularly in multigenerational family enterprises where the interweaving of family and company grows increasingly complex. Their major function is to serve as a link between the family and the company, ensuring that family values are kept while also supporting the profitability and sustainability of the firm.

The preservation of a family's heritage and values is central to the work of a family council. As firms develop and adapt, there is a danger that the original concept may be diluted. The council works hard to ensure that future generations are well-versed in the family's history, beliefs, and vision for the future. This not only instills pride but also fosters a feeling of purpose among family members.

Furthermore, family councils play an important part in dispute resolution. Disagreements in family enterprises are often fueled by familial emotions as well as commercial issues. The council offers a formal forum for open discussion of such concerns, ensuring that they do not cross over into the operating side of the firm.

Another important consideration is succession planning. Family councils often supervise the process of grooming the next generation, ensuring they have the necessary skills and expertise. This proactive strategy guarantees that leadership responsibilities are seamlessly transitioned, reducing any interruptions.

Family councils serve as stewards of the family's heritage while also ensuring that the company thrives. They understand that the success of a family company comes from its unique combination of familial values and professional management, and they work hard to maintain this delicate balance.

### Independent Board Members in Objective Decision Making

Including independent board members in a family business's governance structure may seem illogical at first. Family companies, after all, take pleasure in their close-knit, familial operations. Independent board members, on the other hand, contribute a degree of objectivity, experience, and impartiality that may be crucial for the business's development and sustainability.

One of the initial advantages is the introduction of new viewpoints. While family members may be firmly embedded in the company's conventional traditions, independent board members provide a varied range of skills from many businesses and sectors. This may lead to novel solutions, risk mitigation measures, and new development opportunities that might otherwise be neglected.

Furthermore, their independence guarantees that choices are made on the basis of commercial value rather than family feelings. This is particularly important in instances requiring difficult choices, such as restructuring, layoffs, or shifting corporate strategy.

In addition to neutrality, independent board members boost the company's reputation in the eyes of external stakeholders, including investors, banks, and partners. Their presence indicates that the company is dedicated to professional governance, which may increase stakeholder trust and lead to stronger collaborations and investment prospects.

However, integrating independent members is not without difficulties. Clear communication is required to ensure that they correspond with the family's beliefs and objectives. It is also critical that their introduction be seen as a step toward maturity rather than an incursion into the realm of the family.

While the family-driven ethos remains at the heart of a family firm, the addition of objective governance structures, such as independent board members, may considerably enhance its development trajectory and operational efficiency. Family companies may position themselves for long-term success in an ever-changing market environment by blending familial values with objective commercial expertise.

## Balancing family interests with business needs

### Strategic Decision-Making in Family Firms

Decision-making in family enterprises is sometimes a delicate dance between familial goals and the company's strategic objectives. These organizations are one-of-a-kind in that they must serve two masters: the family and the business. Frequently, what is best for one person may not be best for the other.

The employment of family members is one regular situation that embodies this relationship. Families may feel compelled to incorporate as many family members as possible in their venture. While this may strengthen family relationships and devotion to the organization, it can also result in inefficiencies if these members lack the essential skills or expertise.

In contrast, if the company requires specialized ability, hiring choices may be made that value competence above familial connections. While such actions are advantageous to the corporation, they may be seen as marginalizing family members, perhaps causing rifts.

This equilibrium may also be seen in investments and reinvestments. Family business owners may desire dividends to improve their financial situation. In contrast, the company may need these assets to be reinvested in order to capitalize on growth prospects or handle market obstacles.

The key is to realize that neither the family's interests nor the demands of the company can be ignored. They should instead be harmonized. This might include defining explicit criteria for family employment in order to ensure that people who join the company are both willing and competent. Similarly, investment considerations may include reserving a part for dividends while ensuring that enough is reinvested to drive future development.

Navigating this balance requires open communication in which both the family's objectives and the business's strategic imperatives are openly articulated. It is possible to guarantee that the family feels appreciated and engaged while the company stays competitive and adaptable via mutual respect and understanding.

**Adaptability as a Keystone in Family Enterprises**

Firms must be flexible because of the speed of the business world, reacting quickly to market fluctuations and developing possibilities. This flexibility extends to the responsibilities that family members perform when the demands of the company and the family's makeup change.

During the early phases, family members sometimes wear numerous hats, undertaking a variety of jobs ranging from operations to marketing. However, as the company expands, specialization becomes necessary. Family members must either upskill or move aside to allow for specialized skills, ensuring that the demands of the company are appropriately satisfied.

The difficulty is in handling these changes without producing conflict. For example, a family member who has been in charge of a division may need to delegate authority to an outside specialist. While this is a business choice, it may be seen as a snub or a demotion.

Similarly, when newer generations enter the firm, an inherent conflict exists between the tried-and-true practices of the older generation and the inventive, sometimes disruptive ideas of the newcomers. Although the company may need this new viewpoint to remain relevant, it may be regarded as a threat to the current order.

Thus, adaptability in family enterprises goes beyond market reactions. It entails constantly reassessing and recalibrating responsibilities to ensure that the organization has the appropriate personnel in the correct places. It is about realizing that jobs and the corporate environment are not static.

To find the correct balance, it's critical to foster an atmosphere in which change is not just tolerated but welcomed. This entails cultivating a culture of continual learning in which family members are encouraged to upgrade their skills, as well as a meritocratic ethos in which jobs are determined by competency rather than ancestry. Family enterprises that are adaptable may guarantee that they stay both cohesive as a family unit and competitive as a commercial organization.

CHAPTER 2

# SUCCESSION PLANNING

Succession planning intersects with family legacy and the future direction of a family-owned business. As family companies grow in size, so does the complex web of connections, duties, and expectations. The transition of leadership and management from one generation to the next, if not managed carefully, might jeopardize the business's sustainability, making succession planning essential.

The notion that organizations develop and that the next generation may provide a new perspective, skill set, and vision is at the core of succession planning. This acknowledgment does not diminish the efforts of previous generations but rather builds a development continuum. Regardless of the natural progression, a sudden or unexpected shift may interrupt corporate operations, disturb personnel, and generate uncertainty for stakeholders. Succession planning mitigates these risks by establishing a clear transition route, assuring continuity, and retaining stakeholder trust.

Examining the figures emphasizes the need for succession planning even more. Many family companies do not survive through the first generation, and even fewer survive through the third generation. The absence of a solid succession plan is one of the key causes of this drop. Families who do not prioritize this critical work are often unprepared to deal with unanticipated obstacles such as the abrupt death of a leader, internal family conflicts, or shifting market dynamics.

Another aspect of succession planning is its impact on family unity. A well-structured plan defines roles, duties, and qualifications for leadership positions, reducing the likelihood of disagreements. It provides a forum for open communication in which family members may express their hopes, worries, and expectations, strengthening understanding and collaboration.

Furthermore, succession planning entails providing the next generation with the skills and information required to successfully run the organization. This might include formal schooling, on-the-job training, or even volunteer work. When the next generation feels prepared, and the previous generation has faith in their successors, the transfer is simpler, and the company is better equipped for future problems.

A robust succession plan demonstrates the company's resiliency and long-term vision in today's competitive business climate. Investors, partners, and customers often see family firms that have a well-defined succession plan as more stable and trustworthy, which improves the company's market image.

Succession planning is much more than simply passing leadership; it's about protecting the heritage, guaranteeing business continuity, preserving family unity, and preparing the company for future challenges and possibilities. Given its multidimensional importance, it remains a critical component of effective family company management.

## Importance of succession planning in family businesses

### How Succession Planning Preserves Business Continuity

Many family businesses that formerly thrived failed when the baton was transferred to the next generation, according to business history. The lack of a well-thought-out succession strategy is often at the root of such blunders. Succession planning is more than just ensuring that someone takes over once the founder or current leader steps down; it is also about maintaining corporate continuity.

The corporate world is always changing. Market dynamics change, consumer tastes fluctuate, and technology advances reshape industry norms. In the midst of these external shifts, internal stability becomes critical. This is where succession planning comes in. It acts as an anchor, ensuring that even if the waters are rough outside, the ship stays stable.

A thoughtfully developed succession plan considers not just the technical know-how necessary to operate the organization but also the enterprise's mission, values, and culture. This offers a road map for the successor, not just in terms of operational chores but also in terms of maintaining the spirit of the firm.

Furthermore, companies are not operated in isolation. They include a plethora of connections, including those with workers, suppliers, consumers, and stakeholders. A sudden change in leadership without appropriate planning might harm these ties. Trust and rapport formed over years, if not decades, might be jeopardized. Such hazards are reduced through succession planning. Continuity is ensured by introducing the successor in stages, enabling them to create connections and learn the complexities of the firm.

Succession planning is concerned with the smooth continuation of a legacy rather than the transfer of a person. It is about accepting that, although leaders may change, the spirit and substance of the firm must remain constant.

## The Emotional Landscape of Succession

Conversations on succession planning in family companies often center on operational issues, financial implications, and company strategy. While they are clearly significant, the emotional component of succession is also vital, albeit generally underestimated.

Family enterprises, by definition, combine the professional and the personal. Business choices often have family ramifications and vice versa. This interweaving is particularly visible during successions. The act of handing the leadership baton is an emotionally charged family event as well as a professional shift.

Consider the founder, who has fostered the company from its inception. For them, letting go is like sending a kid to college. There's pleasure in watching it develop, but there's also fear of leaving it in the hands of someone else, even if that someone is their own kid.

The problems for the successor are many. There's the immense responsibility of carrying on a legacy, the pressure to impress stakeholders both inside and beyond the family, and the unavoidable comparisons to their predecessors.

Furthermore, familial dynamics come into play. Sibling rivalry, perceived favoritism, or emotions of being overshadowed may emerge, threatening both family peace and business stability.

As a result, addressing the emotional environment is essential to succession planning. Open lines of communication must be created in order to address concerns, expectations, and goals openly. Individual and family counseling or mediation sessions may be quite beneficial. Periodic family gatherings when business is handled openly may also aid in the development of trust and understanding.

In a family firm, succession means more than simply ensuring that the company has a leader for the future. It's about preserving the family fiber that is inextricably woven into the company tapestry. Recognizing and overcoming emotional complexities is critical to a successful shift.

### The Role of Training and Mentorship

Identifying next-generation leaders is a critical step in the succession planning process. It's tempting to look for leaders that resemble their predecessors. However, as corporate environments change, the leadership necessary for tomorrow may look quite different from what worked in the past. In this setting, cultivating leadership from within via training and mentoring seems to be a smart method.

Family enterprises have an innate pool of tacit knowledge, which is often handed down through generations. They may use this to create organized training programs that are targeted to the unique demands and difficulties of their sector and business model. Such programs have the added benefit of providing necessary skills while protecting the company's basic values and culture.

Mentorship, when combined with training, enhances the learning experience. Potential leaders may be matched with seasoned professionals inside the family or even industry experts from outside the family. They are exposed to a plethora of experiences, tactics, and choices via mentoring, which fosters critical thinking and hone decision-making abilities.

Furthermore, mentoring provides a secure environment for these developing leaders to share issues, seek guidance, and comprehend the complexities of company operations. This symbiotic connection provides them with the knowledge and confidence to take leadership positions when the time comes.

In family enterprises, the route to leadership should not be a quick climb. It should be a steady ascent, assisted by systematic training and reinforced by mentoring, to ensure that when next-generation leaders take the reins, they have not just the talents but also the knowledge to lead successfully.

### Implementing Assessment Tools and Feedback Mechanisms

Next-generation leadership in family firms often faces the issue of reconciling familial sympathies with corporate demands. While connection and heritage are significant, the capability and aptitude of the future leader for the post cannot be overlooked. Integrating objective evaluation tools and feedback channels may considerably improve decision-making.

Personality tests, leadership aptitude assessments, and role-specific skill tests, for example, give concrete data on a candidate's strengths and opportunities for growth. Such assessments aid in determining not just who is ready for leadership today but also who has the potential to develop into the job with the correct mentoring.

Furthermore, 360-degree feedback methods, in which employees get feedback from peers, subordinates, superiors, and, in certain cases, clients, provide comprehensive insights into a candidate's working style, interpersonal skills, and problem-solving approach. Such feedback, particularly when received anonymously, is often frank and may highlight both positive and negative characteristics.

The feedback process does not stop with the selection. Periodic feedback loops after the leadership transfer guarantee that the new leader is aligned with the company objectives adjusts to developing difficulties, and creates a pleasant work environment. It also allows them to adjust their path early in their leadership career.

While family ties are important in company transitions, objective evaluation, and feedback guarantee that leadership selections are based on aptitude and merit; in the long term, this objective approach not only boosts economic success but also reduces the possibility of family strife caused by perceived prejudices or unfair selection procedures.

## Leading Together: Prepping Families & Pros for Success

### Breaking the Familial Barrier

When addressing family company leadership, there is a tendency to emphasize the lineage, sometimes omitting non-family experts. With their outside experiences and distinct viewpoints, these people may offer transforming ideas to the organization. However, in order for them to be genuinely great leaders, they must work in an inclusive workplace that breaks through the family barrier.

The perceived validity of non-family professionals' leadership is one of the most critical issues they encounter. To combat this, family enterprises must aggressively foster a culture in which merit trumps ancestry. Businesses may convey a strong message that leadership is earned through capacity by objectively recognizing and rewarding skills and contributions.

Communication channels that are open play an important part in this dynamic. Interactions between family members and non-family experts on a regular basis develop understanding and reduce the 'us vs. them' mindset. They may establish shared objectives, address issues, and design tactics that cater to the greater vision of the organization via conversations.

Furthermore, shared experiences may significantly deepen these ties. Leadership retreats, team-building activities, and cross-functional initiatives may assist in blurring the distinctions between family and non-family members by focusing on common goals rather than individual backgrounds.

While family companies are built on tradition, they must also be forward-thinking. They not only tap into a larger talent pool by building an inclusive leadership environment, but they also open the path for new ideas that a diverse leadership team brings to the table.

**Catering to Diverse Leadership Aspirations**

One-size-fits-all approaches to succession planning are seldom successful. Family members and non-family professionals each bring their own set of goals, abilities, and problems to the table. Recognizing this variety and developing individualized development routes is critical for future leaders' holistic growth.

For family members, the trip often begins much earlier. As kids get older, they see the complexities of the company and absorb its ideals. Their growth route should capitalize on this innate awareness while also providing formal schooling and external industrial experience. This dual approach guarantees that they respect the company's history while simultaneously providing new insights.

Non-family professionals, on the other hand, may already have industry expertise but need absorption in the company's culture and intricacies. Their training should focus on knowing the company's history, principles, and long-term goals. Mentorship from older family members may be quite beneficial in this situation, providing them with insights that go beyond official training (Kenton, 2022).

It's also important to acknowledge that not every family member wants or should take on leadership positions. Likewise, not every non-family professional wants to be a top-tier leader. Regular check-ins, feedback sessions, and open talks may assist in determining their genuine ambitions and aligning their routes appropriately.

Finally, succession planning is about ensuring continuity and progress. By providing individualized growth pathways, family companies guarantee that every prospective leader, whether from inside or outside the family, is equipped with the proper skills and expertise to move the firm ahead while honoring its history and anticipating future expectations.

CHAPTER 3

# CONFLICT RESOLUTION

The merging of personal ties and professional tasks within the particular terrain of family enterprises may be both a strength and a weakness. Conflict is one of the most serious issues that has arisen as a result of this fusion, making conflict resolution an essential component of family company management.

Arguments in family enterprises are sometimes caused by differences in vision, perceived inequalities, generational gaps, or personal arguments that permeate into the professional world. If left unresolved, these conflicts may fester, threatening not just the business's operational effectiveness but also the family relationships that give many businesses their specific personality.

Conflict resolution is critical in family companies for a variety of reasons. First and foremost, it provides business continuity. Conflicts may cause disruptions in everyday operations, poor decision-making, and even legal conflicts. A well-defined conflict resolution procedure may assist in limiting these risks by ensuring that conflicts are resolved swiftly and do not escalate to the point where the business's existence is jeopardized.

Second, it keeps the family's heritage and reputation alive. A public family dispute or evident internal strife may destroy the company's brand, causing stakeholders, partners, and consumers to lose faith in it. Family companies may preserve the trust and respect they have earned over generations by concentrating on resolving problems graciously and internally.

Finally, conflict resolution encourages creativity and progress. When treated constructively, opposing viewpoints may be a source of innovation, leading to better ideas and methods. Family enterprises may benefit from a variety of opinions by creating a culture in which disputes are seen as opportunities for debate and learning rather than confrontations.

Furthermore, dispute resolution strengthens family members' trust and togetherness. Knowing that there are grievance procedures in place offers family members the confidence to express their concerns without fear of ostracization or reprisal. It promotes a culture of mutual respect, understanding, and cooperation.

Furthermore, successful conflict resolution may act as an example for other workers in the business. When employees witness that disagreements, even among family members, are handled fairly, transparently, and respectfully, it instills faith in the organization's principles and leadership. It establishes a baseline for how conflicts should be handled, fostering a happy working atmosphere.

Conflict resolution in family business management involves more than simply settling disagreements. It's about building a robust firm that can overcome the problems that come with the unique combination of family and business. It's about cherishing and sustaining family relationships while ensuring the business thrives and evolves. Given these enormous repercussions, dispute resolution remains a critical component of good family business management.

## Challenges of conflicts in family businesses

### When Business and Personal Intersect

Conflict is complicated in any commercial context, but in family firms, the merging of business and familial relationships adds an emotional component that may exacerbate problems. While professional disagreements at non-family firms may be driven by strategy or money, choices in family enterprises are often influenced by decades of personal history, shared experiences, and, in some cases, old grudges.

The emotional intensity of these conflicts may often overshadow the root reason for the conflict. A debate over growing the firm, for example, may bring up sentiments of favoritism from childhood or unsolved disagreements from previous years. What began as a business-related disagreement swiftly devolved into a deep-seated family conflict, making settlement much more difficult.

Furthermore, family members have a better knowledge of one another's weaknesses. They may abuse these weaknesses at heated times, leaving scars that endure long after the business problem has been handled. This not only strains the family fabric but it may also lead to judgments based on emotion rather than what is best for the company.

Navigating this emotional minefield requires a keen knowledge of the underlying currents. Open communication, competent mediation, and clear boundaries between family and work duties all become important tools in managing and resolving these emotionally charged conflicts.

**Legacy and Longevity:**

The responsibility to sustain generational legacies is a specific problem encountered by family companies. When disputes emerge, they affect not just current stakeholders but also previous generations and future heirs. The weight of 'what was' and 'what should be' may have a significant impact on 'what is,' adding layers of complication to arguments.

For example, older family members who appreciate traditional practices handed down through generations may be resistant to adopting contemporary technologies. On the other hand, younger members may feel suffocated by what they perceive to be antiquated traditions, causing tension. The argument isn't simply about technology; it's about honoring the past while looking forward.

Similarly, choices regarding broadening the firm, altering its direction, or even rebranding may lead to squabbles exacerbated by the urge to preserve the family's reputation and heritage. Every choice is seen through the prism of years of history, making small disagreements seem huge.

Family enterprises must create a balance in order to solve these problems. It is critical to recognize and appreciate the company's past while being adaptive to the ever-changing business situation. Inclusion becomes critical. Ensure that each generation feels heard and appreciated in order to pave the road for collaborative solutions that honor the past while innovating for the future.

### The Psychological Impact of Familial Roles in Business Conflicts

Individuals often accept roles within the constraints of a family unit, whether by choice, force, or evolutionary conditions. The oldest may be seen as the responsible one, while the youngest may be regarded as the family's free spirit. When family members work together, these roles, formed through years of interactions and experiences, eventually make their way into the commercial arena. While these positions may be beneficial in terms of giving clarity and organization, they can also be a cause of contention.

Consider the following scenario: the youngest member offers an interesting company concept. If this person has always been regarded as the "irresponsible" one, their suggestion may be discarded without thorough examination, not because of the worth of the concept but due to the anticipated family dynamic. Such dismissals may breed animosity and underestimate, widening the gulf of misunderstanding.

Furthermore, family responsibilities may lead to unreasonable expectations. The "responsible" sibling may be continually expected to settle conflicts or bear obligations, which may lead to feelings of exhaustion or being taken for granted. In contrast, if a family member who has always been supportive suddenly wants to head a new initiative, other members may object, not because of competence concerns, but because it upsets the "natural order" of things.

To address this, introspection and potentially external mediation are required. Families in business must be aware of whether they are responding to a proposition because of its intrinsic worth or because of age-old family dynamics. Regular seminars or counseling sessions in which participants analyze and comprehend their positions may prepare the way for more objective, business-focused relationships.

## Guidance on effective conflict resolution

### Embracing Open Dialogue and Vulnerability

Conflicts are especially difficult in the context of family enterprises because of the delicate weave of professional and personal connections. Fostering an atmosphere that values open communication and vulnerability is one of the most important instruments for resolving these issues. Unlike in traditional corporate environments, where conflicts may be kept completely professional, family relationships can mean that emotions run deeper, and previous baggage can impact current issues.

Open communication entails establishing safe places in which every member of the family feels empowered to express problems without fear of retaliation or rejection. This requires a willingness from all sides to genuinely listen and abstain from getting defensive. Often, the underlying sentiments of being devalued or misunderstood are the core reason for a fight rather than the apparent argument at hand.

Along with open communication, vulnerability is essential. Vulnerability entails admitting one's emotions, vulnerabilities, and faults. Admitting a mistake or showing sentiments of pain might be seen as a sign of weakness in a family company. However, it is a strength in reality. Individuals who are vulnerable open the ground for true understanding and reconciliation.

Furthermore, accepting vulnerability entails recognizing when outside help, such as professional mediators or counselors, is required. The intricacies of family relations need the use of an objective third party to lead the settlement process. Overall, fostering an atmosphere that values open discussion and vulnerability not only helps to settle disagreements but also builds family relationships.

### The Role of Structured Mediation in Conflict Mitigation

Structured mediation is an effective method for resolving family business problems. While informal talks have their place, certain issues need a more organized approach to ensure that all sides are heard and a fair resolution is reached.

Structured mediation entails having a neutral third party, often someone with conflict resolution skills, oversee the dialogue. This mediator does not take sides but rather assists in navigating the dialogue so that it stays constructive and does not deteriorate into personal assaults. An objective statistic might be important in the setting of family companies, where emotions often run high.

The procedure begins with each participant uninterruptedly giving their opinion on the topic. This sets the tone and ensures that everyone feels heard. Following that, the mediator assists in identifying areas of agreement and disagreement. The objective is to establish an agreement or, at the very least, mutual understanding via a series of guided talks.

The focus on retaining respect and professionalism makes structured mediation especially successful in family business situations. While family members may have years, if not decades, of personal history, the mediator ensures that the meeting stays focused on the business-related disagreement at hand.

Furthermore, these meetings often finish with action items or directions for avoiding future disagreements, empowering the family company to tackle issues on its own. Structured mediation, in essence, not only resolves the present problem but also fortifies the firm against future conflicts.

# Decisions in Harmony: Family Unity Strategies

## Adapting Transparency as a Pillar of Decision-Making

Transparency is frequently a double-edged sword in the peculiar setting of family enterprises. On the one hand, members' familiarity may occasionally lead to unspoken assumptions and expectations. On the other hand, honest communication is essential for avoiding misunderstandings and possible disputes.

In family companies, transparency is more than simply open financial statements and transparent company goals. It goes further, embracing clarity in roles, duties, expectations, and decision-making logic when family members understand the 'why' behind company decisions; even if they don't always agree, the likelihood of disagreements decreases dramatically.

A transparent culture also reduces the likelihood of distrust. When every family member, regardless of position, has access to critical information, an environment of inclusion is created. This method not only promotes educated decision-making but also boosts the confidence of newer members.

Transparency, however, is not without its difficulties. When sensitive business information is at risk, confidentiality and discretion become critical. It is at this point when creating limits becomes critical. While transparency is essential, it is also critical to guarantee that sensitive data is not exploited or obtained by rivals.

By adopting transparency as a pillar, family companies may guarantee that, while using the benefits of their close-knit relationships, they avoid the dangers of unstated expectations and assumptions.

### Harnessing Mediation to Bridge Gaps in Family Decision-Making

Mediation is a crucial tool in family enterprises, particularly when standard communication methods fail. Family companies are one-of-a-kind entities in which emotions, personal history, and professional stakes all mix, resulting in nuanced disputes that cannot be handled via traditional discussion.

Mediation is the introduction of an objective third party, the mediator, who encourages free conversation between contending parties without forcing solutions. The duty of the mediator is to facilitate the discourse, ensuring that all parties are heard and supporting them in reaching a mutually accepted conclusion.

Mediation may be especially helpful in the realm of family business when decision-making processes stall due to long-standing personal grudges or opposing visions for the organization's future. Because mediators are trained to handle delicate problems objectively, they may assist family members in distancing personal feelings from the business at hand, allowing for a better focus on what is best for the firm.

Furthermore, mediators provide a new viewpoint. Unlike family members who are highly invested in the company and its historical dynamics, mediators approach issues with an open mind. This may aid in the identification of previously undiscovered solutions or new paths for cooperation that family members may have neglected owing to emotional biases or previous experiences (Bautista, 2018).

Family companies that include mediation in their decision-making toolset not only have a higher chance of resolving problems but also of preventing them. Family companies may develop a culture of constructive debate by fostering an atmosphere where open discussion is encouraged and guided by experts, ensuring decisions are made in the best interests of the firm, even when personal disagreements exist.

### Leveraging Emotional Intelligence for Harmonized Decision-Making

Emotional intelligence (EI) is often overlooked in family business decision-making. Emotional intelligence (EI) is the capacity to detect, comprehend, regulate, and react to emotions in oneself and others. EI is particularly more important in the setting of family enterprises when personal and professional connections are strongly entwined.

Being aware of one's own emotions, as well as those of family members, may have a considerable impact on how choices are made and accepted. Recognizing when a family member is reluctant to make a business choice due to unresolved conflicts in the past, for example, might lead to addressing the source of the problem rather than simply its surface appearance.

A high EI also means greater communication. Those who are emotionally aware may manage touchy themes with grace, ensuring that talks stay fruitful rather than devolving into emotionally charged conflicts. This expertise is especially useful at critical decision-making points when the stakes are high, both for the company and for family connections.

Furthermore, building EI within the context of a family company might result in more empathic leadership. Leaders who understand and appreciate their team members' emotions may create a more pleasant, inclusive, and collaborative work environment. Such leaders are also more suited to handle change, resolve issues, and successfully encourage their staff.

Incorporating emotional intelligence training sessions or seminars into family companies may be a smart investment. Family enterprises may guarantee that their decision-making processes are not just productive from a commercial viewpoint but also harmonious and sensitive to the deep human dynamics at play by cultivating a heightened sense of emotional awareness and empathy.

CHAPTER 4

# FINANCIAL MANAGEMENT

Family enterprises, although rooted in history and bonded by intimate personal relationships, are, at their heart, economic concerns. Astute financial management is at the core of their long-term viability and development. The complexities of managing money within a family company framework distinguish it from other corporate entities, emphasizing the significance of customized financial solutions adapted to its specific demands.

Understanding the financial mechanics of a family-run firm necessitates striking a balance between corporate goals and familial duties. Family members' perspectives on dividends, reinvestments, and asset distribution may differ, demanding a defined financial plan. Effective financial management ensures that the company stays profitable while meeting its obligations to family members and other stakeholders.

The necessity for company continuity and long-term development is one of the key reasons financial management is so important. Family companies may negotiate market uncertainties, adapt to changing economic landscapes, and capitalize on growth possibilities by using sound financial procedures such as budgeting, forecasting, and financial risk assessment. Even the most well-intentioned family company might struggle to stay viable without strong financial management, particularly in unpredictable markets.

In addition, financial management is critical in succession planning. When leadership passes from one generation to the next, capital implications typically arise, whether in the form of buyouts, share reallocation, or asset distribution. A well-defined financial plan guarantees that the transition goes smoothly and does not affect the company's operating capital or liquidity.

The function of financial management in maintaining the business's reputation is also important. Transparent financial processes and a track record of fiscal responsibility help to build confidence among suppliers, consumers, investors, and other stakeholders. In an era when corporate responsibility is more scrutinized, a family firm that exhibits good financial management stands out and gains a competitive advantage.

Furthermore, when family companies grow, they may seek possibilities outside of their typical sectors, such as diversification, mergers, or acquisitions. Adroit financial management is critical in such situations. It guarantees that the company's activities are consistent with its financial health and long-term goals rather than overextending or diminishing its basic principles.

While family companies often place a premium on heritage and tradition, they must also remain aware of new financial developments and tools. The adoption of modern financial technology and techniques is encouraged by effective financial management, ensuring that the firm stays relevant and nimble.

In family company management, financial management is a delicate dance between respecting history and guaranteeing profitability. It secures the company's future, protects its reputation, supports expansion, and secures its position in an ever-changing market environment. Given these numerous duties, financial management is unquestionably critical to the success and survival of family-owned businesses.

## Family Business Finance: The Key to Longevity

### Leveraging Long-Term Vision with Prudent Financial Planning

Family firms often take pleasure in their capacity to think in terms of generations rather than economic quarters. This long-term vision, however, must be supported by strong financial planning in order to convert into long-term success. In this perspective, financial planning involves more than simply balancing the books for the year; it is about maintaining the company's economic health for decades if even centuries.

One key benefit that family firms often have is the capacity to reinvest revenues back into the company rather than distributing them to external shareholders. This may lead to long-term growth. However, without smart financial planning, even this advantage may turn into a disadvantage, with cash being funneled into non-productive sectors or being underutilized.

Furthermore, family enterprises often have linked finances, with personal family demands and corporate spending occasionally blending. Effective financial management guarantees that neither the company nor the family's financial health is jeopardized. It also aids in the calculation of equitable pay, dividends, and reinvestments.

Succession is another crucial issue. With several family members possibly participating, precise financial norms and procedures help eliminate possible conflicts over shares, dividends, and control, guaranteeing seamless generational transfers.

Thus, by integrating long-term ambitions with thorough financial planning, family companies may guarantee that they not only survive but prosper, leaving behind a legacy that is strong in both principles and economics.

### Ensuring Liquidity while Maintaining Ambition

Family companies, like other businesses, experience economic downturns, market upheavals, and unexpected hurdles. While desire and a growth mindset are important, securing liquidity is as important in navigating these difficult moments. Financial management is critical to achieving this delicate balance.

Having enough cash on hand isn't enough to ensure liquidity. It is about having assets that can be turned swiftly into cash without incurring severe losses. This might include diversifying one's investment portfolio, keeping clean credit lines, or just adopting wise financial discipline in good times to build a buffer for bad times.

The special difficulty for family firms, though, is to retain liquidity without constraining ambition. With strong roots and personal interests at stake, the risk appetite of a family firm may vary from that of a non-family organization. Businesses, on the other hand, may guarantee they are well-positioned to capture opportunities while still retaining a safety net via intelligent financial management.

Setting away a part of revenues on a regular basis into liquid assets, hedging risks via various investments, or even something as basic as making prompt bill payments to preserve a strong credit score may all make a big impact.

While ambition propels a family business ahead, guaranteeing liquidity via good financial management offers a safety net, enabling the firm to take prudent risks and capitalize on opportunities, assuring long-term development and continuity.

### The Role of Financial Audits in Upholding Trust

The family business ecosystem is distinctive not just in its operational elements but also in the underlying emotions, trust, and human ties that constitute its foundation. While trust is an important component of family companies, assuming it removes the requirement for formal financial control may be a costly mistake. In this situation, financial audits become necessary not just for legislative reasons but also to maintain and strengthen confidence.

Financial audits give an objective assessment of a company's financial situation. This third-party viewpoint guarantees that all stakeholders, whether actively engaged in daily operations or not, have a clear and accurate picture of the financial health of the organization. This openness might help to avoid any misunderstandings or emotions of distrust caused by perceived financial disparities or injustices.

Furthermore, when family companies expand and change, so do their financial complexities. There may be new collaborations, diversifications, or investments in the works that not all family members are aware of. Regular financial audits guarantee that these endeavors are successful, legal, and in keeping with the overall financial plan of the organization.

Furthermore, financial audits might detect inefficiencies or possible sources of cash leakage. For a family company, ensuring that every dollar is accounted for is a question of maintaining family heritage and ensuring that future generations inherit a financially sound corporation.

While trust is the foundation of family businesses, it should be supplemented with openness and responsibility. Financial audits fulfill this function by ensuring that confidence is maintained, misunderstandings are avoided, and the financial health of the organization is not only preserved but also maximized for future development.

## Budgeting and financial planning

### The Interplay of Family Values in Budgeting Decisions

In contrast to their corporate competitors, family enterprises often include personal values, traditions, and familial responsibilities in their financial decisions. Budgeting is an important aspect of financial management since it reflects the family's objectives, ambitions, and obligations.

Budget allocations in many family businesses may favor sectors that have emotional significance or are considered as a family heritage. For example, a certain department, project, or charitable endeavor may get continuous financial allocations because of its historical or emotional value to the family, even if its return on investment is not as great. These financial actions highlight a family's value system, in which profit isn't the only motivator.

On the other hand, family values may be a motivator for monetary responsibility. Prudence, legacy preservation, and forward-thinking may lead to conservative budgeting habits that prioritize savings and investments above current spending. These beliefs may also affect actions such as reinvesting revenues in the firm, supporting family members' educational goals, or putting money away for unanticipated obstacles.

While these value-driven budgeting decisions enhance the culture of the family company, they also need careful balancing. Financial planning is critical in this case, ensuring that family values are upheld while the firm stays financially sustainable, competitive, and growth-oriented. It's a balancing act between respecting the past and being realistic about the present and future, ensuring that the company continues to be a tribute to the family's beliefs through generations.

**Technology for Enhanced Financial Forecasting =**

As the business environment changes, family businesses must compete not just with other family businesses but also with global giants, startups, and technologically sophisticated initiatives. In such a case, depending entirely on conventional budgeting procedures might put family companies at a disadvantage. Enter technologically based financial forecasting.

There are various benefits to using technology in financial planning. To give more accurate financial projections, advanced algorithms can monitor market patterns, anticipate consumer behavior, and assess global economic indicators. This accuracy is critical for family companies to keep ahead of the competition, spend resources more efficiently, and capitalize on new market possibilities.

Furthermore, real-time financial data may assist family companies in reacting more quickly to market shifts. Having real-time information provides for more flexible financial decision-making in the face of rapid market upheaval, a change in customer preferences, or unexpected global events. This adaptability might be the difference between seizing a business opportunity and falling behind.

However, incorporating technology into financial planning is more than simply a matter of keeping competitive. It's also about maintaining continuity for many family enterprises. When younger family members join the company, they bring with them knowledge of technology, sophisticated financial procedures, and fresh viewpoints. Using technology in financial planning may help bridge the generational divide by combining the knowledge of the older generation with the creativity of the younger.

## Managing Financial Risks in Family Enterprises

Any business endeavor entails some level of risk. Financial hazards may have a greater impact on family enterprises since both the family's livelihood and its heritage are at stake. Financial risk management, therefore, becomes about more than just protecting assets; it is also about maintaining the family's legacy and future.

Every company choice, whether it's entering a new market, introducing a product, or incurring debt, has financial ramifications. In the realm of family business, these choices often bore the weight of generations past and future. An ill-timed investment or over-leveraging might risk not just the present status of the firm but also future family members' possibilities.

It's also worth noting that avoiding all risks might limit development and innovation. Understanding, analyzing, and managing these risks is critical. Diversifying assets, providing proper insurance coverage, and hedging against market changes are all examples. It also entails developing open communication channels via which financial plans and their attendant risks may be discussed, debated and settled cooperatively.

Furthermore, the changing global economic scene, which is characterized by fast technical breakthroughs and geopolitical upheavals, poses both difficulties and possibilities. Family companies, which are sometimes steeped in history, must establish a forward-thinking approach to financial risk management. This includes remaining current on global economic trends, comprehending rising market dynamics, and using technologies for predictive financial analytics.

## Financing options and strategies for managing intergenerational wealth

### External Financing to Drive Family Business Growth

Family companies are frequently largely reliant on internal financing sources since they are entrenched in history and heritage. In a volatile company climate, however, leveraging external funding may offer the necessary cash injection to encourage innovation, growth, and competitiveness. External finance encompasses a wide range of options, including conventional bank loans, venture capital, private equity, and, more recently, crowdsourcing. Each of these solutions has advantages and disadvantages, making it critical for family companies to navigate this environment astutely.

Bank loans, the most common kind of external funding, have simple terms and interest rates. Nonetheless, they need meticulous financial paperwork and often include collateral, generally in the form of company assets. On the other hand, although venture capital and private equity are more flexible, they frequently imply giving up some control over the firm. Control and heritage may be a source of contention in many family enterprises. A more recent strategy, crowdfunding, draws into the pooled financial power of the public. It's especially valuable for product-based family companies wanting to gauge consumer interest in new items.

But why should family firms consider seeking outside funding? For starters, it may boost growth without exhausting internal resources. This is particularly important in intergenerational family enterprises where asset preservation for future generations is a top focus. Second, outside financiers, particularly venture capitalists and private equity companies, provide more than simply money. They provide industry knowledge, coaching, and access to a larger network, which may be quite beneficial for traditional family companies looking to modernize.

Family companies, like any other financial choice, must consider the advantages and downsides. It is critical to comprehend the financial arrangements and the long-term repercussions and to guarantee consistency with the company's basic values and goals.

### The Role of Trusts and Estate Planning in Preserving Family Wealth

For family companies, the continuation of wealth between generations is a top priority. It is not just about sustaining financial stability but also about leaving a legacy for future generations to build on. Trusts and estate planning emerge as effective instruments in this quest, providing structured and tax-efficient structures for asset transfer.

Creating a family trust may give several benefits. For starters, it enables unambiguous asset delineation and distribution, guaranteeing that each family member's part is precisely stated. This may considerably lessen possible inheritance conflicts. Trusts can provide tax advantages, particularly in nations where inheritance or estate taxes are high. Families may reduce their tax burdens by putting assets in trust, ensuring that more money is handed down to the next generation.

Estate planning, on the other hand, is a broader strategy that includes wills, powers of attorney, and other legal directions. A well-crafted estate plan assures that, in the case of a family company owner's death, the business moves easily and without legal problems. It also specifies how assets outside the firm, such as real estate, investments, or personal possessions, should be allocated.

However, open communication is essential for these techniques to be successful. All family members should be informed about trusts and estate planning, including their complexities and ramifications. Regular inspections and revisions are also necessary, particularly in the face of changing financial or family situations.

**Family Business Debt Management**

The delicate dance of family company management adds tremendous subtlety to the balance between debt and equity. For family companies, debt may be a double-edged sword. On the one hand, it may offer the necessary funds for growth or to fill operational shortages. Excessive or badly managed debt, on the other hand, may strain relationships, risk the company's future, and imperil the riches and legacy intended for future generations.

Recognizing the psychological and emotional consequences of debt in family companies is the first step in understanding its particular dynamics. Unlike corporations, where choices are often made exclusively on financial parameters, family companies must contend with emotions and familial relationships. A debt incurred as a result of a family member's choice may carry a great emotional burden and, if not handled properly, can lead to friction on both the commercial and family levels.

Furthermore, in family enterprises, stakeholders are sometimes the same as stockholders. This overlap complicates debt management since failing on a loan or facing bankruptcy is more than simply a company failure; it may put the family's financial well-being in jeopardy. This mixture demands a strong and well-planned debt management approach.

Clear communication and openness are essential for effective debt management in family companies. It entails informing all stakeholders on the reasons for incurring the debt, its potential advantages, and the repayment plans in place. It's also critical to keep family funds separate from corporate finances to keep personal assets safe from commercial threats.

CHAPTER 5

# HUMAN RESOURCES

Managing human resources (HR) in a family company has a unique mix of problems and possibilities. The intertwining of family connections with professional positions adds levels of complexity to HR operations, making it a critical component in the smooth operation and development of family businesses.

First and foremost, human resources are critical in defining the lines between family and company. Personal ties and professional tasks may overlap in family enterprises, which, if not handled carefully, may muddy borders and lead to problems. HR is responsible for ensuring that roles and duties are clearly defined, performance is properly assessed, and any possible biases are addressed intentionally.

HR assumes responsibilities for talent management and succession planning, highlighting its significance.

Transitioning positions through generations or among family members in a family company needs sensitivity and planning. HR ensures that family members get adequate training, that their skills are refined, and that their responsibilities are effectively matched to their competencies. Recognizing and cultivating non-family talent inside the company is also crucial. Because their contributions and progress are critical to the company's success, talent retention, and development are critical HR activities.

Another important factor is the development of organizational culture. Family enterprises can have strongly embedded values, traditions, and convictions. Human resources ensures that these principles are continually preserved, conveyed, and ingrained in all members, family and non-family alike. Employees have a feeling of identity, pride, and belonging as a result of this consistent culture, which drives engagement and loyalty.

Furthermore, dispute resolution, a recurring subject in family companies, often comes within the jurisdiction of human resources. Personal conflicts may flow over into work settings and vice versa. Effective human resource policies may anticipate possible squabbles, resolve conflicts, and guarantee that disagreements are handled constructively, protecting both the business's integrity and family unity.

As family companies change and grow, they often need the incorporation of current HR practices and technology in order to remain competitive and efficient. This includes everything from applying modern personnel management tactics to integrating innovative HR technologies for easier operations. As a result, HR serves as a link between the company's past and its future, ensuring that, although the organization stays entrenched in its principles, it does not shy away from innovation.

Human resources are more than simply recruiting, payroll, and assessments in family company administration. It is about creating a balanced atmosphere in which family traditions and professional achievement coexist. It is about assuring continuity, propelling development, and sustaining the distinct character of family businesses. The significance of human resources in family enterprises cannot be overstated, given its diverse function. It is still a driving factor in the company's long-term success.

## Complexities of managing employees in family businesses

### Integrating External Professionals into a Family-centric Culture

Bringing in outside expertise into a family firm has its own set of obstacles and possibilities. Traditions, shared histories, and enduring customs are often at the heart of family company culture. While this strong culture provides stability, it may also operate as a barrier to outsiders, possibly leading to a sense of 'we against them.'

Many external specialists encounter the initial obstacle of deciphering the informal communication networks inside the family company. These networks often function on the basis of common familial histories and backgrounds, which an outside professional may not be aware of. In the lack of this intimate information, misunderstandings or misinterpretations might occur.

Furthermore, in family enterprises, familial bonds may often have a greater effect on decision-making than professional hierarchy. Navigating these entangled ties might be difficult for an outside expert. In a family company environment, decisions that seem reasonable and clear in a traditional corporate setting may be overlaid with familial factors.

However, it is not all difficulties. External experts provide family companies with a new viewpoint. They are responsible for introducing new approaches, challenging established paradigms, and driving innovation. Their position as an outsider permits them to raise questions that family members may avoid owing to established conventions or to avoid disagreement.

Family enterprises must be proactive in order to incorporate external specialists effortlessly. It is critical to have clear communication about roles, expectations, and decision-making structures. It is also critical for family members to be open to new ideas and prepared to adapt and change. After all, the combination of family dedication and external competence may be the recipe for long-term development.

**Professional Development in a Familiar Environment**

Professional development inside a family company provides a unique quandary. Unlike traditional firms, whose development paths are more open and organized, family enterprises often function inside a complicated web of connections and emotional ties that may occasionally overwhelm meritocratic norms.

A family company employee, whether a family member or an outsider, may find their career path impacted by forces beyond their control or performance. For example, a family member may be offered a leadership job based on ancestry rather than merit, or an external employee may reach a plateau because the next leadership position is 'is 'and 'is reserved' for a family member.

Despite these complications, family enterprises provide several prospects for professional advancement. Because of the close-knit character of such organizations, workers, even at low levels, are often exposed to essential company operations and decision-making processes. In the long term, this broad exposure may be a big benefit, offering essential expertise.

A few tactics may be used by family companies to encourage growth and professional development. To begin, drawing a clear line between family and company might be beneficial. This entails basing business choices on merit rather than family relationships. Second, investing in ongoing learning and development may guarantee that all personnel, whether family or external, have access to the necessary skills and information.

Establishing mentoring programs in which seasoned family members teach younger workers may also be a method to share expertise while boosting development. Such measures not only help workers but also guarantee that the company thrives beyond generations.

### Engaging and Retaining Non-Family Talent in a Family-Oriented Business

Keeping non-family talent in a family firm might be especially difficult. Such workers often struggle with the perception of being an 'outsider' in a close-knit group, which may have an impact on their sense of belonging and job happiness. They may also perceive restricted prospects for advancement, feeling that crucial leadership jobs are reserved for family members.

Non-family personnel, on the other hand, provide tremendous value to the organization. Their outside opinions, uncolored by family dynamics, may provide new insights and impartial perspectives. They often bring particular talents and knowledge to the table, addressing gaps in the company's capabilities.

It is critical for family companies to develop an inclusive atmosphere in order to engage and retain non-family personnel. This includes making certain that all choices, including promotions and awards, are based on merit rather than familial connections. Equal growth possibilities must also be provided, maybe via well-defined career routes and professional development programs.

It is also critical to integrate non-family personnel into the corporate culture. Team-building exercises, mentoring programs, and frequent communication forums may help with this. Non-family personnel are more likely to remain committed when they feel appreciated and see a clear future for themselves inside the company, bridging the gap between family and non-family talent for the benefit of the company.

## Hiring practices and criteria

### Incorporating Family and External Talent

Hiring methods become a delicate activity within the fabric of family enterprises, particularly when reconciling the demands for familial engagement and external expertise. Hiring from inside the family provides its own set of benefits, most notably an intuitive awareness of the company's basic principles and culture. A family member may also show a stronger devotion by comprehending the implications and complexities of the tradition they are protecting. However, depending only on family might prevent the company from broadening its talent pool and lead to significant skill shortages.

External employees, on the other hand, provide new ideas and specialized experience and may be critical in fostering innovation. Their impartial, objective viewpoint, uninfluenced by family dynamics, may often lead to unbiased, objective judgments that propel the organization ahead. However, integrating them might be difficult, particularly if the dominant culture is excessively insular.

The idea is to maintain a careful equilibrium. Transparent hiring criteria that prioritize both talents and cultural fit may help family companies determine whether to hire from within and when to hire from outside. Regular talent audits may indicate shortages that may be best addressed by hiring from outside sources. Moreover, establishing a clear, merit-based route to leadership positions may inspire both family and non-family members to give their all, knowing that their achievements will be rewarded.

### Integrating Traditional Values with Modern Hiring Techniques

The deep-rooted history and principles that many family companies preserve are one of their distinguishing features. These often have an impact on their employment procedures, causing companies to favor trustworthiness, loyalty, and long-term commitment. While these are undeniably significant characteristics, focusing only on them might stymie the adoption of more data-driven and methodical recruiting practices.

In today's competitive environment, successful recruiting goes beyond personal preferences. Psychometric exams, structured interviews, and skills testing are changing the way firms evaluate prospective applicants. They provide objective information on a candidate's ability, cultural fit, and prospective areas for development. This is particularly useful for family enterprises since it allows them to separate personal prejudices from professional judgments.

However, it is critical for family companies to adopt these strategies while maintaining their own character. For example, while conducting structured interviews, they might include questions on alignment with family values. Similarly, when utilizing evaluation tools, they might highlight characteristics that align with the company's culture.

**Professional Development within Family-Owned Enterprises**

In the world of family enterprises, it is common to wrongly believe that professional growth and development are automatic, based purely on genealogy. However, in today's commercial environment, more than simply a common surname is required for success. There is a strong need for systematic professional development inside family-owned firms, whether an employee is a family member or an external recruit.

Professional development in this context accomplishes numerous essential goals. For one thing, it guarantees the company's competitiveness. Employees must be taught the newest best practices and technology as industries grow. This training extends beyond external employees; family members must also be prepared with the most up-to-date information in order to lead successfully.

Furthermore, systematic professional development may be used to increase retention and morale. Family companies, like any other firm, confront the difficulty of keeping outstanding employees. Offering opportunities for advancement and upskilling may make a difference, making workers (whether family or not) feel appreciated and involved in the company's future. Furthermore, it eliminates the inherent problems of complacency and entitlement, particularly among family members who may believe their positions are safe simply by virtue of birth.

As a result, family companies must take a proactive approach. These businesses can ensure they have a workforce that is not only loyal due to familial bonds but also because of a shared vision for business excellence by organizing regular training sessions, encouraging attendance at industry conferences, or even facilitating higher education for promising employees.

## Employee development and fostering a positive workplace culture

### The Heartbeat of Family Business Longevity

A dedication to ongoing learning is at the core of any successful family business. While history and heritage are important components of many businesses, it is the unwavering desire for development and adaptability that secures their long-term viability. This applies not just to the growth of company concepts, goods, or services but also to personnel development.

Employees in a family firm sometimes wear numerous hats, going above and beyond their job duties. This needs a diverse skill set, which can only be developed via ongoing learning activities. Businesses guarantee that their staff stays nimble and adaptive by investing in programs that provide training on the latest industry trends, technical tools, or even soft skills. This is especially important for family members who may one day take on leadership responsibilities. A well-rounded education that covers all aspects of the industry is essential for them.

Continuous learning promotes inventiveness in addition to skill gain. Employees who are exposed to a variety of fresh ideas and approaches become excellent at thinking outside the box, resulting in unique solutions and offers that may differentiate the company in a competitive market.

Furthermore, a commitment to learning sends a powerful statement about the importance the company takes on its personnel. When employees, whether family or non-family, see that their personal development is connected with the success of the firm, it develops a feeling of loyalty, devotion, and togetherness.

### The Role of Workplace Culture in Bridging Generational Gaps

Family companies are special in that they often include many generations working together. The generational difference is evident, with founders still actively involved in decision-making and passionate Gen Z members ready to make their imprint. While this brings in a diverse range of viewpoints, it may also lead to possible confrontations. This is where a strong, healthy workplace culture comes into play.

A strong workplace culture is more than mission statements on a wall; it is a living thing that governs interactions, choices, and behaviors inside the firm. It fulfills the twin objective of respecting traditions while opening the way for modernization in the context of family companies. Businesses may guarantee that every voice, regardless of age or seniority, is respected by instilling values such as respect, open communication, and teamwork.

Mentor-mentee interactions may be very beneficial. Combining experienced family members with younger entrants promotes knowledge transfer, ensuring that the wisdom of the past is effortlessly interwoven with the vitality and fresh insights of today.

Regular team-building activities and open forums may also help to boost camaraderie. Employees who participate in activities outside of their usual area of work help to break down formal hierarchies and foster real connections. This togetherness becomes the company's strength, enabling it to face obstacles front on. After all, the family is at the core of every family company, and a healthy workplace culture guarantees that this relationship continues unbroken through generations.

CHAPTER 6

# BUSINESS GROWTH AND INNOVATION

Family companies, which are often seen through the perspective of history and heritage, are not immune to the demands of development and innovation. In reality, these two factors are inextricably linked, assuring the survival and relevance of family businesses in an ever-changing economy.

Striking the correct balance between preserving time-tested habits and adjusting to new market realities is a major problem for many family companies. The significance of corporate expansion cannot be emphasized. Even the most established family firm faces stagnation, loss of market share, or becoming outdated in the face of agile competition if it does not expand. Growth guarantees not just financial sustainability but also chances for the next generation, ensuring the business's intergenerational continuation.

Growth, on the other hand, is insufficient. The growth's direction, methods, and sustainability are all critical. This is when creativity comes into play. In a family company, innovation extends beyond product or service advancements. It includes innovative ways to consumer involvement, entering new markets, using cutting-edge technology, and even rethinking the company's basic principles and operating structures.

The value of innovation in family company management is multifaceted. For starters, it permits the company to remain relevant. Businesses that fail to innovate risk alienation in an era of fast technical breakthroughs and evolving customer tastes. For family businesses, innovation bridges the gap between their rich heritage and the needs of the modern market.

Furthermore, innovation often leads to increased operational efficiency. Whether it's employing digital technologies for improved inventory management or using data analytics to streamline supply chains, creative methods may drastically improve a company's bottom line. Such efficiencies may be game changers for family firms, which often work with close-knit teams and lean structures.

Furthermore, innovation fosters a culture of constant learning and flexibility. It inspires family members of all ages to be interested, open-minded, and forward-thinking. This not only encourages intergenerational cooperation but also guarantees that the company is constantly ready to capitalize on new possibilities.

Expansion and innovation increase the brand's attractiveness to external stakeholders. Investors, partners, and even consumers want to work with companies that have a clear vision for the future and the flexibility to reinvent themselves.

Business development and innovation are more than just buzzwords for family businesses; they are lifelines. While a family business's origins may be in its illustrious history, its future is unquestionably dependent on its capacity to expand and innovate. Embracing these two pillars guarantees that the family business's history not only survives but grows, leaving a mark on new frontiers while keeping entrenched in its core beliefs.

## Necessity for family businesses to adapt

### Tradition as a Springboard for Modernization

Family companies, with their rich tapestry of history and heritage, are often seen as traditional stalwarts. This tradition, on the other hand, is not only a monument to their lasting character, but it may also be a powerful motivator for modernity. The trick is to recognize that tradition is not about keeping stagnant but rather about utilizing the past as a compass while navigating the future.

The tales, attitudes, and lessons ingrained in family company history provide significant insights. They serve as cautionary stories, highlight crucial decision-making moments, and emphasize the necessity of perseverance. When navigating uncharted territory, this rich mine of insight comes in handy. For example, if a family firm encountered a crisis three decades ago and successfully navigated it, reviewing that incident might provide techniques for dealing with current issues.

However, although history may provide direction, adaptation demands a forward-thinking perspective. This includes adapting to technology developments, broadening product portfolios, and entering developing markets. This might imply incorporating ecological methods or investigating internet sales channels for a family-run textile company. The trust and reputation that family companies have built over decades help with this shift. Customers who recognize the brand's history are more inclined to accept its present incarnations.

Although a family business's heart beats with history, its pulse must sync with the rhythms of the modern world. Family companies can guarantee they stay not just relevant but trailblazers in their particular areas by exploiting their unique historical vantage point and connecting it with modern-day expectations.

**External Pressures and Opportunities**

Change is the one constant in the fast-paced world of business. These developments often bring with them a unique combination of demands and possibilities for family enterprises. External variables, such as economic upheavals and regulatory changes, as well as changing customer tastes and technology improvements, have a substantial influence on the operating environment.

Take a look at the world of consumer preferences. Businesses, particularly family-owned ones, are under pressure to embrace eco-friendly practices as global awareness swings toward sustainability. This is more than simply a nod to external pressures; it also represents a chance to tap into a growing market of mindful customers. Similarly, with the digital revolution affecting every aspect of the company, from marketing to operations, family companies are at a crossroads. Given their typical operating styles, they might either see this as a hindrance or an opportunity to reach global audiences and simplify procedures.

Regulatory changes are also important. As governments throughout the globe tighten their grip on compliance, taxes, and ethical standards, family companies must adapt. This may need restructuring, rethinking company methods, or hiring legal advice.

However, these external forces bring with them extraordinary potential. The globalized world provides opportunities for family companies to extend beyond their local boundaries, form worldwide relationships, and innovate in their product and service offerings.

## Strategies for business expansion and diversification

### Family Values in New Ventures

When a family firm decides to grow or diversify, it brings a particular combination of traditions, values, and history with it. These factors might be critical in distinguishing new initiatives in a crowded market. Family values, in particular, may act as a guidepost, ensuring that expansions are not only financially sustainable but also in line with the essential essence of the organization.

Consider a long-established organic farm owned by a family. As public awareness of health issues grows, the family may consider branching into the production of organic health foods or drinks. Their background in organic farming provides a distinct selling point in this case. Consumers are more interested than ever in the narrative behind their goods. This farm doesn't simply offer organic juice; it sells juice founded on years of sustainable agricultural techniques.

Similarly, a family-owned bookshop may branch out into digital publishing. While using current technologies to reach a larger audience, they may preserve their devotion to handpicked material, perhaps highlighting books that correspond with the family's interest in certain genres or themes.

While family values are an asset, they should not limit creativity. It is critical to find a balance between sticking to basic ideas and adapting to the modern economy. Regular family councils may assist in striking this balance, ensuring that all members, young and old, have a role in the new venture's future.

As family companies diversify, they benefit from a long history and a set of principles. When used effectively, these may not only secure the success of new businesses but also fill them with a depth that connects with customers.

**Joining Forces for Growth**

Collaborative enterprises are another possible method for development and diversity. These may be mergers, acquisitions, or strategic collaborations with other businesses that complement the services of the family company. Collaborations enable organizations to combine resources, share risks, and more effectively enter new markets.

For example, a family-owned textile company may cooperate with an emerging designer, resulting in a unique combination of traditional textiles and modern patterns. This not only diversifies the product line but also presents the company to a new clientele, all while maintaining the brand's essential essence.

Collaborations, however, provide their own set of obstacles, particularly for family firms. It is critical to ensure that the collaborating company has comparable beliefs and ambitions. Misalignments may cause disagreements, degradation of brand identity, and even operational difficulties.

It's also critical to establish clear limits and duties from the start. This is particularly important when working with non-family firms since decision-making dynamics might vary greatly. Legal contracts that explicitly define duties, responsibilities, profit-sharing arrangements, and departure plans might help to avoid possible problems.

Additionally, open communication is essential. Regular meetings between stakeholders, openness in operations, and mutual appreciation for each entity's capabilities may all help to establish a good partnership.

Although partnerships are attractive, they need careful preparation and attention, particularly for family enterprises. When done correctly, they may catapult the company to new heights by providing options for diversification that would be difficult to attain on its own.

### Harnessing Digital Transformation for Diversification

In an age where technology is driving corporate operations and customer interactions, family companies seeking to expand and diversify must embrace digital transformation. The digital arena provides several opportunities for family companies to explore new markets, simplify operations, and improve customer experiences, driving development and diversification.

E-commerce is one method of diversification. Family companies may expand their reach beyond regional boundaries by developing an online presence and tapping into a worldwide consumer base. A firm may use an internet platform to expose its goods or services to a larger audience, enhancing brand exposure and perhaps generating greater sales. This change, however, requires a well-planned digital marketing strategy that focuses on developing brand identity, engaging consumers, and maximizing online sales channels.

Adopting new technology such as Artificial Intelligence (AI) and data analytics may also help businesses grow. These technologies allow family companies to gain knowledge about customer behavior, market trends, and operational efficiency. A family-owned restaurant chain, for example, might utilize data analytics to determine popular menu items, peak business hours, and consumer preferences, allowing educated choices to be made to optimize the menu, manage inventory, and improve customer satisfaction.

Furthermore, digital transformation promotes product and service innovation. Family companies may explore new business strategies, launch innovative products, and improve current services by utilizing technology. A family-run crafts firm, for example, may use 3D printing technology to make personalized goods that suit unique consumer demands while also opening up new income sources.

While the advantages of digital transformation are many, it is critical for family companies to proceed with prudence. To successfully traverse the digital world, it is critical to analyze the business's digital readiness, invest in relevant technology, and upskill the staff. To guarantee a seamless balance of tradition and innovation, technology integration should be linked with the business's values, objectives, and consumer expectations.

## Fostering innovation and staying competitive

### Multigenerational Knowledge for Innovative Breakthroughs

Multiple generations often operate side by side in family enterprises. This one-of-a-kind framework combines experiences, perspectives, and abilities, resulting in a reservoir of information that can be used to drive innovation. The combination of traditional expertise from older generations and new insights from younger members may stimulate inventive discoveries, guaranteeing the company's competitiveness.

Senior family members' expertise, gained through years of industry experience, gives a profound grasp of key company principles, long-standing customer connections, and time-tested operating practices. Their insights on previous achievements and mistakes may provide vital lessons, serving as a basis for fresh ideas.

Younger family members, on the other hand, often provide exposure to current industry trends, technology breakthroughs, and shifting customer habits. They may bring modern ideas, such as digital marketing tactics, e-commerce models, or long-term business practices that are in line with market needs. When joined with their elders' core knowledge, these new ideas may lead to comprehensive developments that honor the company's heritage while preserving its relevance in the present market.

However, using intergenerational knowledge requires open communication lines throughout the organization. Regular brainstorming sessions, knowledge-sharing seminars, and inclusive decision-making forums may help to enable a smooth interchange of ideas across generations. It is critical that all family members feel appreciated and heard in order to develop a culture of creativity.

Furthermore, this collaborative approach fosters a feeling of shared ownership and responsibility for the company's progress. By combining the talents of older and younger generations, family firms may create new solutions that are both traditional and forward-thinking, assuring long-term success in a volatile business market.

## Building External Collaborations to Drive Innovation

To remain competitive in today's fast-paced corporate climate, more than just internal innovation is required. Collaborations outside of the family unit are often the key to groundbreaking inventions. Family companies may get access to new technology, broaden their product offerings, and penetrate uncharted areas by forming strategic partnerships and alliances with other groups.

Collaborations may take many different forms. Collaborations with technology providers or startups may assist traditional family companies in digitizing their operations, incorporating sophisticated analytics, or implementing AI-driven solutions. These technology advancements may help family companies compete by streamlining operations, improving product quality, or improving customer experiences.

Collaboration with academic institutions may also help with research and development. Universities and research institutes are often at the front of scientific progress. Family firms may collaborate with them on cutting-edge research initiatives that will result in product developments or enhanced production practices.

Diversification may also be achieved via joint partnerships with complementary firms. A family-owned textile company, for example, may cooperate with a fashion designer or a technology firm to create smart clothes. This cooperation may result in new product lines, new consumer groups, and new income sources.

However, although external cooperation has many advantages, it also has certain drawbacks. It is critical to align goals, maintain consistent communication, and manage any conflicts of interest. Before engaging in partnerships, family companies must perform extensive due diligence to evaluate the possible risks and advantages.

Furthermore, it is critical to protect the family business's basic principles and identity. Collaborations should add value to the company's services without diminishing its core. External partnerships may push family companies onto new development trajectories with a balanced strategy, ensuring they stay inventive and competitive in a constantly developing market.

## The Power of Data for Competitive Strategy

Data has evolved as one of the most significant assets for organizations in the digital era. Understanding and leveraging data might be the key to preserving competitiveness and guaranteeing long-term sustainability for family businesses. Every transaction, contact with a consumer, and simply a visit to a website creates data. When properly examined, this data may provide important insights into corporate operations and market trends.

For example, sales data may tell which goods are the most popular, when they are popular, and who they are popular with. This data may be used to guide stocking choices, marketing initiatives, and even product development. Similarly, consumer comments and reviews may reveal areas for development, ensuring that the firm is always evolving to suit the demands of its customers.

Predictive analytics can also foresee future trends. This may involve anticipating weather trends to choose which crops to sow for a family-owned agriculture company. Forecasting fashion trends based on web search data might be a task for a retail company.

The sheer amount of data, on the other hand, might be intimidating. It is critical to invest in tools and abilities that allow you to cut through the noise and concentrate on what is important. Hiring data scientists or using sophisticated analytics technologies may be necessary. It is also critical to verify that data gathering and analysis are conducted in accordance with privacy laws and ethical standards.

While data provides useful insights, it is critical to combine data-driven judgments with intuitive understanding gained from years of business experience. The mix of empirical data and experience may give a comprehensive perspective of the corporate environment, influencing strategic choices.

## CHAPTER 7

# EXIT STRATEGIES

Exit plans are a crucial component of sound company planning despite the fact that they are often ignored in the emotionally charged environment of family enterprises. Even while many family businesses have the goal of lasting forever, there are times when both external and internal circumstances need a change in strategy, which in turn necessitates a methodical approach to disengagement.

One of the most important aspects to take into account is the possibility that not all younger family members or potential successors would have the same enthusiasm or perspective about the company. An exit plan gives clarity and direction for such instances, ensuring that the value of the firm is maintained and that family members are not obligated to an operation they no longer desire to lead.

In addition, family enterprises, just like any other kind of enterprise, are sensitive to the dynamics of the market. The course of a corporation may be drastically redirected by factors such as the economy, upheavals in the sector, or pressure from competitors. In situations like these, having an exit plan that is clearly outlined may offer a buffer, enabling family owners to sell or step back from their businesses without suffering excessive financial or reputational harm.

In addition, it is essential to have an exit strategy in place in the event that there are disputes or conflicts within the family on the route the firm should go. Rather than allowing disagreements to fester and possibly harm both family connections and the firm, a pre-decided exit strategy may give a path for settlement, assuring the continuance of the business or its orderly breakup. This is preferable to the alternative of allowing disagreements to fester.

The relevance of an exit strategy in terms of asset preservation and financial planning for the family is something that is sometimes disregarded by business owners. Family companies are often responsible for a significant percentage of the wealth that is accumulated by a family. Having a well-defined exit strategy protects this money from being lost due to unanticipated successions or sudden departures from the market. Instead, it offers a plan for taking cash out of the investment or reinvesting it, guaranteeing the family's continued financial stability.

Exit plans are very important for the management of a company's legacy, even beyond the financial concerns involved. An exit strategy guarantees that the family's values, brand equity, and reputation are maintained, even if they are no longer managing the day-to-day operations of the firm. This may be accomplished via the transfer to new management, the merger with another corporation, or the sale of the company.

In addition, exit plans have a part to play when it comes to external interactions. Knowing that there is a backup plan gives peace of mind to business partners, investors, and even important personnel. Because of this, they are able to approach their interactions with the family company with the knowledge that any unanticipated events have been planned for and taken into consideration.

Even if the idea of "exit" may seem contrary to the everlasting ethos of family companies, the very fact that a plan has been developed and is being implemented is a credit to foresight, accountability, and savvy management. The unquestionable significance of exit plans in the overall administration of family-run businesses cannot be overstated. These strategies provide clarity, protect a family's heritage, and assure financial security.

## Various exit strategies for family business owners

### Ensuring Business Continuity Through a Well-Planned Succession

One of the key worries of many people who run family businesses is making certain that their company will continue to exist and be successful after they have left it. When it is done correctly, succession planning has the potential to act as a strategy for a phased leave and to assure the continuation of the firm. The most important aspects of succession planning are the identification and preparation of potential successors, whether those successors come from within the family or from outside the family.

The transfer of control of a company is not the only aspect of a successful succession. It entails transmitting the information, abilities, and culture of the organization from the current leader to the one who will succeed them. This process may take many years, during which time the individual who will succeed the present leader will work alongside that person to get an understanding of the nuances of the firm, its operations, the competitive environment, and the issues that are specific to the organization.

Other stakeholders, such as workers, suppliers, and customers, need to be aware of the change and prepared for it in order for there to be a smooth transition. A sudden change in leadership that is not preceded by any previous notification might give rise to worries about the stability of the organization, which may be detrimental to both business relations and operations. Such worries may be alleviated via open and honest communication, which also helps to maintain the faith of stakeholders.

In addition to this, crucial factors include financial concerns. The proper preparation of a succession may help avoid the possible negative effects of tax consequences and liquidity concerns. It is also vital to have detailed legal paperwork outlining the transition process, particularly when numerous family members are involved, in order to avoid future conflicts. This is because of the nature of the transfer.

In summary, a well-planned succession makes it possible for a business owner to sell their company with the confidence that it will be taken care of by knowledgeable people, that it will be positioned for future expansion, and that the legacy they have created will be respected and carried on.

**Preserving Legacy and Wealth through Strategic Business Sales**

It's not always easy to make the call to sell the family company, whether in whole or in part. However, there are circumstances in which this departure plan is the most practical option. This is particularly the case when there is no obvious successor in sight or when the future prospects of the business are unclear. The most important thing is to make sure that the owner's heritage is protected and that the sale maximizes wealth.

It is essential to have a solid understanding of the worth of the company before ever contemplating selling it. For this purpose, a full company valuation is required, one that takes into account intangible assets, the value of the brand, market position, client base, and possible future profits. If you want an accurate estimate and to make sure your expectations are met, you might consider hiring specialists to carry out an objective review.

The following phase, which comes after the value has been determined, is to locate prospective purchasers. These may include other competing businesses, bigger corporations on the hunt for strategic acquisitions, private equity groups, or even wealthy individuals. Especially in situations when the family name is strongly tied to the firm, it is of the utmost importance to make certain that the prospective purchaser shares the same values and vision as the business.

There is some leeway in the terms of the transaction. If the owners of a company want to protect the reputation of their company and its heritage, they have the option of choosing conditions that prevent the buyer from making significant changes to the brand or from laying off a significant number of employees. Those who are more concerned with the money element may choose to concentrate on guaranteeing a one-time lump-sum payout or negotiating advantageous conditions for staged payments.

Having legal representation throughout this procedure is quite beneficial. In order to safeguard the interests of the seller, each and every facet of the transaction, from non-disclosure agreements to the actual sales contract, must be subjected to stringent legal examination.

The choice to sell a family company is a weighty one, both emotionally and monetarily. However, if done properly, it has the potential to be a successful departure plan that respects the legacy of the company owner while also ensuring that their fortune is maintained for future generations.

### Embracing Business Liquidation with Grace and Strategy

A family firm may find that going out of business via liquidation is the best workable exit plan in certain circumstances. Although it may seem to be a choice of last resort, liquidation may really be a smart decision. This is particularly true in situations when the company is confronting issues that cannot be overcome or when the market circumstances have made the business model outdated.

The sale of a company's assets, followed by the settlement of its obligations and, finally, the distribution of any leftover assets to the company's shareholders, is what happens throughout the liquidation process. This procedure, which often marks the conclusion of the journey that the firm has been on, maybe emotionally draining for family-owned companies because of its significance. However, if the plan for liquidation is carried out correctly, it is possible to guarantee that all stakeholders, including members of the family, obtain the most possible value.

It is very necessary to acquire a comprehensive value of the company's assets before moving on with the liquidation process. This includes both tangible and intangible assets, such as patents, trademarks, and the value of the brand. Physical assets like equipment, real estate, and inventories are included in this category. It is possible to get the greatest prices for these assets with the employment of professionals (Garcia, 2023).

During the liquidation process, it is essential to settle any remaining obligations. This includes reaching a settlement with the company's creditors, resolving any outstanding legal concerns, and guaranteeing compliance with all regulatory obligations. This method may be made more organized and effective by using a staged approach and putting the most pressing obligations at the top of the priority list.

## Implications of selling the business

### Valuation Complexities in Family-Owned Ventures

The process of valuing any company requires a combination of art and science, but the number of variables that must be considered increases significantly when dealing with businesses that are owned by a family. The worth of the company is not just determined by its measurable assets and profits; rather, it is intricately entwined with the heritage of the family, the reputation of the brand, and sometimes even non-economic characteristics that have been cultivated over the course of many generations.

When it comes to the company's finances, family firms could have assets that aren't accounted for in the conventional balance sheets. These might include intellectual assets such as recipes, processes, or customer lists that have been handed down through generations, as well as tangible goods such as an ancestral property that is utilized as the site of a company. The valuation has to take into consideration assets of this kind, particularly if they make a substantial contribution to the revenue of the company.

Then, there is the worth of the brand. A customer base that is difficult to define may be enjoyed by a family-owned firm, particularly one that has been operating in the same industry for many generations. The worth of the company may be greatly increased as a result of intangible assets such as trust, recognition, and goodwill that have been built up through time. But how exactly can one quantify emotion or the amount of a customer's loyalty?

The dynamics that occur inside family companies add an additional layer of complexity to the valuation. The obvious delineation of financial boundaries may get muddled when there are loans or financial favors given by family members to one another, unofficial profit-sharing arrangements, or even unregistered investments. Additionally, many choices in family companies may be motivated more by emotions than by the need for financial prudence. One example of this would be keeping a legacy unit that is not operating well because of the emotional value it has. The process of arriving at an objective appraisal might be complicated by factors such as these.

However, it is essential to do a thorough appraisal, not only for the family that is selling the property but also for prospective purchasers. It prepares the ground for future talks and ensures that all parties have a clear understanding of the nature of the transaction that is taking place. Engaging the services of professional valuation specialists, particularly those with expertise in managing family companies, may give a balanced view and bridge the gap between emotional worth and market value.

**Legacy Preservation Post-Sale**

When considering the sale of their family firm, one of the most significant challenges that family business owners face is determining how best to protect their heritage. Even if the financial components of a deal are clearly important, it is just as important, if not more so, for many people to make sure that the ethos, values, and reputation of the family are not compromised in any way after the sale of the business.

A family's legacy in the world of business is an entity with several facets. It manifests itself in the goods or services offered, the manner in which the company engages with the community in which it operates, the way it treats its workforce, and even in the one-of-a-kind customs and tales that it upholds. The anxiety caused by the possibility that a new owner would fail to respect these elements can be overwhelming.

Including language in the purchase agreement that specifies which terms and conditions are not open to negotiation is one strategy for addressing this issue. For instance, if the company has a history dating back a hundred years of hosting community events, a provision might assure that this practice would continue for a certain amount of time after the sale of the firm.

Another thing that causes anxiety is the possibility of the company changing its name or branding following the purchase. If the family name has become inextricably linked with the company, dropping it may seem like wiping out generations of history. It is possible for buyers and sellers to negotiate conditions under which the old brand name will continue to be used, either alone or in combination with the new brand.

Employees, particularly those who have been associated with the company for a significant amount of time, are important bearers of the heritage of the company. The preservation of legacies may be advanced by stipulating in contracts that purchasers will be afforded equitable treatment after the sale of their property.

Despite the fact that contractual terms provide a legal framework, the most important part of legacy preservation is selecting the appropriate buyer. It is more probable that the legacy will be maintained by a buyer who has the same values as the company, who is familiar with its history, and who appreciates its past. Therefore, the intangible alignment of ideals becomes a vital aspect of such transactions and should not be overlooked in favor of quantitative measurements.

## Passing the Torch: Prepping for Next-Gen Business Transition

### Developing Leadership Skills in the Successor

When passing down a family company to the next generation, it is just as important to prepare the next generation to take over as it is to prepare the firm itself. The succession process goes more swimmingly and is more likely to be successful when the replacement is prepared for leadership roles and given the required tools.

Leadership, in contrast to management, places an emphasis on persuading others to follow, encouraging the development of teams, and determining the culture of a company. This often entails taking on the responsibility of inheriting a heritage, gaining a grasp of the core values that the organization has upheld throughout its history, and guiding the team toward achieving future objectives. Training for future leaders may start early, enabling potential successors time to progressively build up their self-assurance and earn the respect of their peers.

The atmosphere of a family-owned firm offers a setting that is unlike any other for the development of leadership skills. In the first place, it is absolutely necessary for the potential successor to have first-hand experience working in a variety of company divisions. This not only deepens their grasp of the company as a whole, but it also gives them the opportunity to cultivate connections at all levels of the organization.

The importance of having a mentor cannot be overstated. The existing leader, who has a lot of experience, may serve as a mentor to others who want to take their place by sharing their insights, the obstacles they've faced, and the solutions they've found. This mentor-mentee connection typically goes beyond professional borders in family enterprises, which makes it richer and more meaningful than other types of mentor-mentee relationships.

It is also quite important to acclimate the successor to other business settings outside the company. This might involve pursuing more education in business, gaining experience via internships in a variety of fields or industries, or working briefly for a new company. These kinds of experiences provide the successor with a new point of view new ideas, and widen their field of vision.

Feedback is a powerful tool that may be used for the development of leadership skills. Regular feedback meetings, in which the successor's actions, choices, and plans are examined, might provide enlightening insights for the future. It is essential that these sessions be productive and put an emphasis on personal development and education.

The growth of an individual's character is an essential component of effective leadership. Emotional intelligence, resiliency, the ability to negotiate, and vision are among the qualities that are just as important as commercial acumen. Developing these skills could benefit from participation in workshops, seminars, or even personal coaching.

Leadership development is a continuous process that, when adapted to the setting of a family company, may help guarantee that the successor not only inherits the firm but also gracefully carries forward its heritage.

**Ensuring Business Continuity During Transition**

The process of passing down a family company to the subsequent generation is a critical step, and it is of the utmost importance to maintain commercial operations during this time. No matter how meticulously a transition is prepared, there is always the possibility that workers, stakeholders, and customers may experience some degree of anxiety. Instilling confidence in others and preparing the groundwork for the leadership of one's successor may be accomplished by making sure activities run smoothly.

The first thing that should be done is to establish a comprehensive transition strategy as far in advance as possible. This plan needs to specify deadlines, milestones, and particular duties for both the leader who will be stepping down and the leader who will take over. To eliminate the possibility of responsibility duplication or voids, positions must be well-defined.

The key to a seamless change is clear and consistent communication. Concerns among internal teams may be alleviated by the provision of regular information about the transition process, timetables, and any prospective changes in the organizational structure. In addition, developing personal relationships with the company's most important stakeholders, customers, and business partners may help to reassure such individuals of the reliability and consistency of the enterprise.

The emotional side of transitions is one component that is often disregarded. It may be difficult for workers who have worked closely with the existing leader for a significant amount of time to adjust to a new style of leadership. To address this issue, you will need to have a combination of training sessions, open house talks, and even therapy sessions at times.

Maintaining a stable financial position during the transition period is essential. It is recommended to maintain a financial buffer to ensure that any possible hitches in operations do not transfer into financial issues. This may be done by ensuring that enough funds are set aside. This may include delaying the completion of significant investments until after the transition is over or ensuring that reserve money is set up and ready to go.

The identification and elimination of any operational redundancies should be a priority. For instance, if there are procedures that are entirely dependent on the present leader, it is imperative that these responsibilities be transferred to a group or the successor as soon as possible. It is possible to ensure that the company will not experience any operational issues as a result of the leader's diminished presence by developing and documenting standard operating procedures, training teams, and creating standard operating procedures.

CHAPTER 8

# LEGAL AND TAX CONSIDERATIONS

Family companies are firmly anchored in human ties and shared experiences, they function within a legal and financial framework. As a result, legal and tax issues are critical in ensuring that the firm not only grows but also complies with regulatory norms, therefore protecting its history.

To begin, knowing and adhering to regulatory requirements is critical for every organization, but it takes on particular relevance for family-run enterprises. Given the family dynamics at work, areas such as ownership arrangements, partnership agreements, and succession planning often combine personal ties with legal obligations. Navigating these waters without a clear legal framework may result in disagreements, which can impair both the operational effectiveness of the firm and family unity. A solid legal framework guarantees that everyone's duties, obligations, and rights are properly stated and understood.

In addition, when family companies expand and adapt, they may consider diversifications, acquisitions, or foreign expansions. Each of these projects carries with it its own set of legal complexities. Failure to address these issues might subject the company to liabilities ranging from financial fines to reputational harm. Understanding and abiding by legal laws on a proactive basis guarantees that the organization may capitalize on possibilities without unanticipated legal entanglements.

Tax effects run parallel to legal concerns. Family companies, by definition, encompass numerous generations, diverse ownership arrangements, and, in certain cases, cross-border activities. Each of these aspects has tax consequences. Effective tax planning ensures that the firm stays financially sustainable and that family members profit to the greatest extent possible from their involvement with the organization.

Tax issues are especially important during transitions, such as transferring the torch from one generation to the next. Such occurrences may result in tax obligations, which, if not anticipated, might put a burden on the company's resources. Furthermore, with authorities throughout the world amending tax legislation on a regular basis, remaining up-to-date and compliant becomes even more important.

Legal and tax factors play an equally significant role in safeguarding the company's image. Businesses are being scrutinized by stakeholders, regulatory organizations, and the general public in an era of increased transparency and corporate responsibility. Any lapse in legal or tax compliance may ruin the family business's image, affecting consumer confidence and market status.

Legal and tax issues in family company management are more than just administrative boxes to complete. They are the foundation of responsible and sustainable corporate operations. These issues are critical in guaranteeing job clarity, allowing seamless transitions, improving financial health, and maintaining reputation. They weave a complicated web of familial connections and commercial imperatives, emphasizing their unquestionable relevance in the effective administration of family businesses.

## Unique legal challenges faced by family businesses

### Ownership Structures and the Intricacies Involved

Family firms sometimes run on generations-old foundations, making their ownership structures more complicated than those of normal corporations. Different family members may have differing degrees of shares in these entities, which may be allocated over time via inheritances, weddings, or strategic business choices. Understanding the complexities of such combinations is critical, particularly when considering the legal implications.

The dilution of ownership is a prevalent problem that arises from these setups. The once-clear division of ownership may become unclear as family trees grow and new people inherit shares. This may lead to a lack of clarity about decision-making power, particularly if the company hasn't expressly specified any decision-making processes. If such issues are not handled, they may lead to internal disagreements and even legal problems among family members.

Furthermore, family enterprises may sometimes depend on informal agreements rather than legally enforceable contracts. For example, a brother may oversee a certain business section based on linguistic knowledge. However, in the lack of formal documentation, such agreements may become points of conflict, especially when revenues or losses are generated by that specific sector.

Another complex issue is the legal ramifications of recruiting procedures inside family enterprises. Preference for family members over perhaps more competent outsider applicants may create ethical questions regarding nepotism. While family members may naturally hold many positions of leadership, maintaining openness and fairness in hiring and promotions becomes critical to prevent any legal difficulties.

Another area fraught with complications is the intertwining of personal and company money. Family members may mistake firm assets for extensions of personal assets, resulting in improper utilization or distribution. Such activities may have tax consequences and may even result in charges of mismanagement or embezzlement.

While family companies benefit from trust-based operations and deep-seated devotion, the convoluted ownership arrangements may provide distinct legal issues. Addressing these issues early, with clarity and foresight, may help to avoid possible conflicts and guarantee the smooth functioning of the organization.

### Balancing Personal Relationships with Contractual Obligations

A network of personal ties is at the core of every family company, frequently taking priority over formal contracts. While trust is the foundation of such businesses, the shifting barriers between personal relationships and professional commitments may provide unique legal issues.

One point of conflict among family members is the execution of contracts. Consider the following scenario: one family member fails to fulfill a contractual responsibility to another, maybe due to unexpected circumstances. While the offended individual may have legal action, doing so may strain personal connections and potentially cause long-term rifts within the family.

Furthermore, estate planning gets complicated, particularly when corporate and personal assets are mixed. Succession planning, which is critical for the smooth continuation of the organization, often necessitates legal paperwork that delineates the transfer of ownership and management responsibilities. However, it is critical to ensure that such changes are fair and do not generate family strife.

Furthermore, confidentiality agreements in family enterprises provide specific issues. While such contracts may be enforced without much emotional baggage in professional settings, personal connections in family companies may make people more slack about such commitments. Breaches, whether deliberate or unintentional, may result in legal ramifications while also undermining family trust.

Salary, bonus, and dividend negotiations are another area that requires caution. While market rates and performance indicators normally decide these in ordinary firms, personal expectations and perceived equity play a key influence in family enterprises. Balancing these feelings with contractual duties might be a legal balancing act.

### Inheritance Laws and Business Continuity

The succession of family enterprises sometimes necessitates negotiating complex inheritance regulations. Every country has its unique set of inheritance rules, and these laws may have a significant impact on the succession process of a family business. Many families' purpose, however, is to assure the seamless continuance of their company heritage, even when confronted with potentially disruptive legal limits.

Inheritance rules in many legal systems require equitable distribution of assets among heirs. This may be difficult for family companies, particularly if not all heirs are interested or devoted to the firm. Such divides may dilute the company's ownership, making decision-making procedures more difficult or perhaps leading to disputes among successors with various ideas for the company's future.

Furthermore, inheritance tax might be a barrier. Transferring assets, especially company shares, may be costly in certain countries. These taxes, if not accounted for, may put a burden on the firm's finances, sometimes prompting the sale of assets or sections of the company to satisfy the tax debt. Such events might impair corporate operations and possibly jeopardize the enterprise's viability.

When family enterprises operate across borders, legal obstacles develop. Different nations' inheritance laws and tax regimes differ. Understanding and preparing in accordance with these many standards is critical for international family companies. Failure to do so may result in legal problems, double taxes, or the unintentional dissolution of corporate units.

Despite these obstacles, many family firms handle inheritance rules effectively to maintain corporate continuation. They do this by proactive legal preparation, which often entails the formation of trusts, holding corporations, or specialized share structures that match with their succession objectives. Family companies may avoid possible interruptions and maintain their legacy by working with legal specialists and analyzing the long-term effects of inheritance legislation.

## Strategies to minimize tax liabilities

### Optimizing Corporate Structures for Tax Efficiency

A main method used by family companies to reduce tax liability is the design and execution of an efficient company structure. The idea of this method is to structure the firm in such a manner that it minimizes taxable revenue via legal routes, taking advantage of various tax rates, incentives, and reliefs available in various countries.

Family enterprises often operate across several industries and geographies. They may guarantee that money is directed via locations with the most advantageous tax regimes by establishing separate businesses for varied activities. A family firm, for example, may develop its intellectual property holdings in a nation with advantageous patent box tax regimes. This allows for reduced taxation on patent earnings, improving overall tax efficiency.

Furthermore, holding corporations are used to optimize company structures. Holding corporations may concentrate ownership and management of many operational firms under the umbrella of the family company. They may be established in countries with advantageous tax treaties and dividend income exemptions, guaranteeing the least amount of tax leakage when earnings are funneled upwards.

Inter-company transactions between the holding company and operational businesses potentially give tax planning options. Transfer pricing, or the price at which goods and services are traded across businesses in the same company group, may be arranged to move profits to lower-tax countries. However, it is critical to verify that these prices are at arm's length in order to avoid violating international tax standards.

While optimizing company structures is a powerful instrument for tax reduction, it is also a difficult one. Family companies must keep current on the shifting tax environments in all of the countries in which they operate. To prevent conflicts and fines, they must also ensure conformity with international tax regulations.

## Leveraging Tax-Deferred Growth Opportunities

One tried-and-true method for reducing tax payments is to take advantage of chances that enable income or capital to develop tax-free. By deferring the tax point, family companies may profit from compound growth, increasing their value before any tax is payable.

The utilization of retirement funds is a popular practice. Many countries provide tax breaks for contributions to retirement plans. The monies in these programs may then grow tax-free until they are withdrawn. Family enterprises may establish pension plans for their workers and family members, ensuring that maximum contributions are made to take advantage of this tax-deferred growth.

Another approach is to choose assets that provide tax-deferred returns. Certain bonds or insurance products enable interest or returns to grow without being taxed right away. Placing a portion of a family business's holdings in such instruments may result in considerable tax savings in the long term.

Real estate investments may also provide tax-deferred growth. Many countries let capital gains be rolled over from one property investment to another, delaying the tax point to a later period. Family enterprises may build their wealth without incurring immediate tax consequences by consistently reinvesting in real estate.

However, although taking advantage of tax-deferred growth possibilities has specific benefits, it also requires planning. Family enterprises must prepare for the future tax point by developing methods to lessen the effect when the deferred tax gets due.

## Utilizing Estate Planning to Reduce Inheritance Tax

Estate planning is critical in reducing the tax burden on wealth handed down to future generations within a family company. Inheritance or estate taxes may have a significant effect, perhaps necessitating the sale of corporate assets to fulfill tax liabilities. However, with careful preparation, family companies may guarantee that their heritage is preserved and that the following generation is not saddled with significant tax burdens.

To begin with, trusts are a common way of estate planning. By putting assets under a trust, the original owner may dictate how they are used or transferred, typically avoiding direct inheritance and the related tax ramifications. Trusts may be set up to benefit individual family members, charity organizations, or even to ensure company continuation. Furthermore, some forms of trusts may remove assets from a person's taxable estate, minimizing the inheritance tax burden.

Another effective estate planning approach is gifting. Many countries enable people to give a specific amount of money to others without paying gift or inheritance taxes. A family company owner may dramatically lower the amount of their taxable estate by gradually giving assets or sections of the firm over time, ensuring that more of the wealth is passed on intact.

Life insurance plans have also found a home in strategic estate planning. When a family company owner dies, a well-structured life insurance policy may offer liquidity, guaranteeing that there is enough money to satisfy any impending inheritance tax bills without the need to sell firm assets.

The value of the firm itself is important in terms of inheritance tax considerations. Family enterprises might possibly minimize the basis on which inheritance taxes are computed by getting a clear and favorable value of the company assets and ensuring that this valuation is approved by tax authorities.

## Compliance with local and international business laws

### The Labyrinth of Local Business Laws

Understanding and abiding by local company rules is critical for any organization, but particularly for family enterprises strongly anchored in local communities. Family companies, which are often defined by traditions and time-honored procedures, may find themselves in conflict with changing legislation. Local company laws may include a wide range of topics, such as labor rights, environmental rules, health and safety regulations, and licensing requirements, to mention a few.

One of the difficulties that family companies confront in this respect is the possibility that personal connections and long-standing habits may clash with formal legal obligations. For example, hiring family members in jobs that need no credentials or failing to keep conventional work hours owing to family obligations may violate labor rules.

Furthermore, family companies, particularly those that have been in operation for generations, may be located in regions that are now classified as ecologically sensitive or protected. As a result, adherence to environmental regulations becomes critical. Local environmental rules may have a considerable influence on enterprises working in areas such as agriculture, fishing, or industry.

Another issue to be concerned about is licensing. With rules always changing, companies must remain up to speed on any licensing changes or requirements to ensure they are operating within legal frameworks. Family enterprises, especially those in specialized industries such as food manufacturing or craftwork, must keep their licenses up to date at all times.

Adherence to local company regulations not only eliminates legal ramifications but also improves the business's reputation in the community. It exhibits professionalism and a dedication to fair and ethical standards, all of which are necessary for establishing confidence and consumer loyalty.

### The Complexities of International Business Regulations

Many family firms are growing beyond their local borders to tap into worldwide markets in an increasingly globalized world. While this provides a significant opportunity for expansion, it also creates the issue of knowing and complying with international business rules.

Different nations have different regulatory regimes, and what is common behavior in one may be prohibited in another. For example, although giving is a standard business practice in many cultures, it may be considered bribery and, hence, unlawful in others.

Another critical factor is trade rules. Family companies that export products must be familiar with the destination country's customs charges, tariffs, and import limitations. Noncompliance may result in heavy penalties and perhaps trade prohibitions in the future.

In recent years, data protection and privacy legislation have grown critical. If a family company handles data from overseas consumers, it must comply with the data protection laws of other countries. Regulations such as the EU's General Data Protection Regulation (GDPR) have extraterritorial application, which means that organizations located outside the EU may still be held accountable for violations.

Furthermore, cultural and ethical factors are important. Family enterprises must ensure that their procedures are culturally appropriate and do not harm local feelings accidentally. Beyond the legal repercussions, such blunders may irreparably harm a company's brand.

CHAPTER 9

# CASE STUDIES AND BEST PRACTICES

Case studies and best practices serve as useful compasses in the complex world of family company management, leading organizations through problems, highlighting paths to success, and providing insights into possible pitfalls. Their significance is complex because they combine theoretical frameworks with real-world applications, providing realistic blueprints for managing the specific obstacles of family businesses.

At its foundation, case studies provide tales of real-world enterprises, recording their adventures, choices, and results. These stories provide comparable situations for family companies, offering insight into how other firms have dealt with difficulties such as succession planning, dispute resolution, and company development. The benefit is twofold: first, they give practical ideas drawn from genuine experiences; second, they foster a feeling of camaraderie, underscoring that issues experienced are not unique but shared throughout the landscape of family-run companies.

Furthermore, these case studies serve as knowledge warehouses. Mistakes and lessons experienced by other family firms become instructional moments, helping organizations to address prospective difficulties ahead of time. Success stories, on the other hand, may inspire and provide replication procedures, ensuring that the wheel does not need to be reinvented every time a stumbling block occurs.

Best practices supplement case studies by distilling the core of effective family business management into tangible methods. These traditions, which encompass time-tested techniques and approaches, often originate from trends noticed across numerous successful family enterprises. For example, how to best instill professional management in a family company or how to effectively incorporate next-generation members into the business fold.

Best practices may also be used as a guideline for family companies. Businesses may find opportunities for improvement by comparing their operations to recognized best practices, ensuring that they function at peak efficiency and effectiveness. Furthermore, these approaches often combine ideas from experts, academics, and industry leaders, integrating objective assessments and suggestions into the complex tapestry of family company operations.

Another critical function of case studies and best practices is as discussion starters. They may serve as a catalyst for family talks, prompting appraisals of present processes, imagining future trajectories, or even reconciling different viewpoints within the family nexus.

Case studies and best practices in family company management are more than simply a collection of tales and suggestions. They are mirrors that reflect the diverse experiences of family businesses, lighthouses that guide ships through stormy seas, and catalysts for reflection and conversation. In a world where human emotions and economic imperatives collide, these instruments provide clarity, inspiration, and direction, highlighting their vital role in the voyage of family enterprises.

## Real-life examples of successful family businesses

### Case study-1: The Resilience and Evolution of the LEGO Group

The narrative of LEGO, a Danish family-owned enterprise, is one of endurance and creativity. Ole Kirk Christiansen founded LEGO in 1932 as a modest carpenter's factory creating wooden toys. The name of the firm is taken from the Danish phrase "leg godt," which means "play well."

By the 1950s, the company had moved away from wooden toys and toward plastic toys, creating the now-iconic LEGO brick in 1958. LEGO's focus on a system of creative play was created under the leadership of Ole's son, Godtfred Kirk Christiansen, paving the way for the interconnecting bricks that sparked children's imaginations worldwide.

However, LEGO's path has not been without difficulties. In the early 2000s, the firm was on the verge of bankruptcy owing to an over-extension of its brand into sectors such as theme parks and intricate toy sets that diverted attention away from its primary product. The company's fortunes were turned around by the prompt intervention and restructuring launched by the third-generation family member, Kjeld Kirk Kristiansen, and then by recruiting an outside CEO, Jrgen Vig Knudstorp.

The concentrate on its core product, simplifying operations, and forging relationships with popular brands like Star Wars and Harry Potter were critical to LEGO's revival. Today, LEGO is a monument to the importance of knowing one's heritage while being adaptable to change, a model from which many family companies may benefit.

### Case study-2: The Endurance and Global Appeal of L'Oréal

L'Oréal, the world's biggest cosmetics and beauty corporation, is an enthralling case study of a family business's evolution into a worldwide behemoth. L'Oréal was founded in 1909 in a modest room in Paris by Eugène Schueller, a young chemist who invented a pioneering hair color recipe.

Schueller's inventive approach extended beyond product creation. He believed in advertising and went door-to-door in Paris to pitch his hair color to hairdressers. His entrepreneurial mentality established the groundwork for what would become L'Oréal.

Under the direction of Schueller's daughter, Liliane Bettencourt, the firm extended its product line and started its worldwide conquest in the later part of the twentieth century. Recognizing the need to meet a variety of beauty demands, L'Oréal pursued a multi-brand strategy, acquiring recognized businesses from across the globe.

L'Oréal's devotion to research and development has been one of the keys to its success. With the concept that "the future of beauty is scientific," the firm spends substantially on research, resulting in breakthroughs that keep it at the forefront of the market.

Furthermore, the company has shown a great awareness of worldwide marketplaces. It does not take a one-size-fits-all approach to beauty. Instead, L'Oréal customizes its products to meet the varying beauty standards and demands of various cultures and areas. This global-local strategy has been critical to the company's global appeal.

The Bettencourt family retains a large interest in L'Oréal, despite the fact that it is no longer actively governed by the founding family. The company's path from a Parisian flat to a worldwide brand demonstrates the ability of family enterprises to achieve massive success while remaining true to their fundamental beliefs.

**Case study-3: The Pioneering Journey of Ford Motor Company**

The story of Henry Ford's Ford Motor Company, which began in 1903, exemplifies the spirit of creativity as well as the struggles and achievements inherent in family companies. Henry's ambition was simple yet transformative: provide inexpensive vehicles for the public. He achieved just that with the Model T, which debuted in 1908. Ford revolutionized manufacturing by introducing assembly line production in 1913, guaranteeing that vehicles were no longer a luxury for the wealthy but were affordable to the common American.

Henry's leadership style was frequently authoritarian, yet he had a clear vision. By the 1920s, Model Ts accounted for half of all automobiles in the United States. This accomplishment, however, was not without its difficulties. Ford's loyalty to the Model T started to erode as rivals began producing vehicles in a variety of colors and designs.

In the 1940s, Henry Ford II, Henry Ford's grandson, took over the corporation. His tenure saw the debut of famous vehicles like the Mustang, as well as a recovery in the company's fortunes. Despite internal family feuds and external corporate obstacles, Ford has shown amazing resilience.

While the Ford family owns a lower part of the corporation now, their impact is apparent. Their devotion to innovation, as seen by their entry into electric cars, is shaping the company's future. Ford's journey demonstrates a unique combination of vision, flexibility, and long-lasting family influence.

**Case study-4: The Legacy and Expansion of Walmart**

Walmart's meteoric rise from a single cheap shop in Rogers, Arkansas, in 1962 to become the world's biggest retailer is nothing short of astounding. Walmart's founding concept, conceived by Sam Walton, was simple: provide lower pricing and excellent service. This customer-focused strategy laid the groundwork for what would become a retailing powerhouse.

Sam Walton's conviction was based on the importance of hard labor, humility, and a constant emphasis on the client. Under his guidance, the Walmart Supercenter was introduced in the 1980s, solidifying the company's retail supremacy.

The voyage, however, was not without its difficulties. Walmart encountered challenges when it started its worldwide development, ranging from adjusting to local market tastes to negotiating intricate international legislation. Nonetheless, Walmart expanded and adapted under the leadership of Sam's heirs, notably Rob Walton as chairman.

Recognizing the shifting realities of retail, one of Walmart's significant evolutions has been its shift into e-commerce. Acquisitions like Jet.com demonstrate the company's intention to compete in the digital era.

While the Walton family is no longer active in day-to-day operations, they continue to shape Walmart's strategy and culture. Their charitable endeavors, particularly via the Walton Family Foundation, demonstrate their dedication to giving back, an ideal instilled by Sam Walton himself.

Studying Walmart's history may provide family companies with insights into the strength of a strong fundamental vision, the importance of flexibility, and the tremendous influence of long-lasting family values on a company's culture and direction.

## Insights Unveiled: Lessons from Case Studies

**Lesson Learned from Case study-1:**

The rise, collapse, and victorious rebirth of the LEGO Group is not just a tale about toys but also a lesson in corporate flexibility and foresight. LEGO began as largely a manufacturer of wooden toys. Recognizing the possibilities of a new material—plastic—the firm moved its major emphasis in the late 1950s and produced the LEGO block. This was a crucial turning point that underscored the need to be open to new technologies and materials, even if they differ from existing processes or products.

The route, however, was not always paved with gold bricks. By the early 2000s, LEGO was on the verge of going bankrupt. Their fast development into other fields, such as theme parks and intricate toy sets, moved them away from their core competencies. The major point here is the need to know one's own capabilities and avoid expanding into areas outside of the company's competence, even if they seem profitable.

However, LEGO's recovery approach is a case study in and of itself. They refocused on their core product, incorporated feedback from their user base into product development, and maintained an unshakable dedication to quality. They also welcomed licensed collaborations, such as Star Wars and Harry Potter, which proved to be a brilliant move. This emphasizes the necessity of working together, leveraging brand equity, and listening to your customers.

**Lesson Learned from Case study-2:**

One of the most important lessons learned from L'Oréal's journey is the importance of research and development. L'Oréal made significant investments in this area, resulting in advances that kept the firm ahead of its competition. Their adherence to science also guaranteed high-quality goods, increasing client confidence.

Furthermore, L'Oréal's growth approach included not just joining but also comprehending a market. They tailored their goods to different beauty standards throughout the world. Their goods for the Asian market, for example, vary significantly from those for the European or American markets. This localization within a global context highlights the importance of cultural subtleties being understood and respected.

Another subject of study is L'Oréal's acquisition strategy. Rather than simply assimilating acquired companies into the L'Oréal mold, they enabled them to preserve their own identities while benefitting from their existing brand value. This demonstrated a knowledge that the value of a brand may often be found in its uniqueness.

**Lesson Learned from Case study-3:**

The path of Henry Ford's Ford Motor Company is a monument to ingenuity, vision, and endurance. One of the first lessons learned from Ford's journey is the transforming power of ideas. At a period when vehicles were considered a luxury for the wealthy, Ford imagined a future in which automobiles were affordable to the general public. His ambition to accomplish this goal resulted in the Model T, a low-cost automobile that changed transportation.

Ford also stressed the need for efficiency in corporate operations. The corporation used the assembly line manufacturing process, which resulted in much higher production rates and lower costs. This technique became a norm not just in the automobile industry but also in other industries, stressing the impact of new operational tactics.

Another important lesson is to be adaptable. Ford has experienced several problems throughout the years, ranging from economic downturns to shifting market expectations. The company's capacity to pivot, rethink its strategy, and adapt to changing circumstances, on the other hand, assured its sustained relevance and supremacy.

**Lesson Learned from Case study-4:**

Walmart's rapid growth from a single Arkansas bargain shop to one of the world's biggest retail companies provides several lessons. Sam Walton's idea was simple but powerful: provide people with cheaper costs and exceptional value. This focus on value for money became the cornerstone of Walmart's strategy, emphasizing the significance of understanding consumer demands and designing a business model around them.

Walmart's expansion also emphasizes the significance of strategic growth. While the firm started with a single shop, its methodical approach to expanding, learning local markets, and changing its methods was critical to its worldwide success. This educates firms about the importance of cultural sensitivity and localization in global marketplaces.

Furthermore, the Walton family's drive to constant innovation has been critical, whether in supply chain management or in incorporating technology into their retail strategy. It teaches us that, although fundamental principles are important, ongoing modernization and innovation are also necessary to remain ahead in a competitive market.

CHAPTER 10

# ETHICAL AND SOCIAL RESPONSIBILITY

Family Businesses, which are typically braided with strands of history, values, and heritage, have an innate viewpoint on ethical behavior and social responsibility. Their approach to business is rooted in family values and long-term vision, and it extends beyond profit-generating. The focus on ethical and social responsibility becomes even more important in this scenario, changing not just the economic landscape but also the larger societal fabric.

Ethical behavior in family companies reflects the underlying beliefs of the family. It includes everything from how they interact with their workers and customers to how they manage conflicts and possibilities for development. Maintaining ethics protects the company's reputation and ensures reliability in the eyes of stakeholders. Furthermore, in an era when customers are growing more aware of company practices, ethical behavior may be a strategic differentiator, promoting brand loyalty and customer trust.

Beyond individual company operations, ethical behavior in family firms sets the tone for the sector as a whole. Given their typically prominent positions in local economies and sectors, family firms may set a good example by encouraging fair procedures, opposing malpractice, and advocating for openness. This ripple effect has the potential to raise industry standards and level the playing field for all players.

The notion of social responsibility supplements ethical concerns. With their extensive neighborhood links, family companies typically have a natural feeling of giving back. This takes many forms, including charity activities and community involvement programs, as well as ecologically friendly practices and inclusive employment rules. Such activities not only benefit society but also strengthen the relationship between the company and the community, creating goodwill and mutual respect.

In addition, social responsibility activities may be strategically connected with commercial goals. A family farm, for example, may invest in sustainable agricultural techniques, which not only improve the environment but also secure the long-term survival of their activities. Similarly, programs focused on education or skill development may foster future talent pools, thereby contributing to the growth and sustainability of the organization.

Ethical and social responsibility are not simply add-ons to the magnificent tapestry of family company management; they are woven into the very fabric of their existence. Family companies safeguard and strengthen their history by advocating ethical standards, ensuring that their brand stands for trust, integrity, and honor. They weave themselves into the fabric of the community via social responsibility, maintaining the symbiotic link between economic success and societal well-being. Together, these pillars highlight the fundamental importance of family companies as guardians of values and agents of beneficial societal effect, not merely as economic entities.

## Ethical considerations in running family businesses

### A Family Business Ethical Dilemma

Family enterprises often confront the issue of aligning commercial goals with ethical concerns. While this is a problem for all organizations, it is more acute for family businesses because they are profoundly entrenched in human ties and family values. The conflict develops when these ideals may be compromised for financial gain or competitive advantage.

A good example is the acquisition of goods or raw materials. Because they provide economic benefits, family firms may get enmeshed in supplier networks that abuse workers or disregard environmental issues. In such instances, the family must decide if it is ready to trade ethical ideals for financial gain. Making the ethical decision may result in short-term financial pressure, but it strengthens the company's brand and creates trust with customers and partners in the long run.

Nepotism is another source of worry. While it is normal for family enterprises to hire relatives, an ethical quandary emerges when these family members are put in jobs for which they are unqualified or are given preferential treatment. This might result in a disillusioned staff, stifling the company's development and creativity.

Family companies may improve their image and preserve their longevity by adhering to ethical procedures. Operating ethically may lead to enhanced brand loyalty, improved stakeholder connections, and a healthy corporate culture, all of which are critical for a family business's longevity and success.

**Upholding Trust in Family Enterprises**

The innate trust between family members is one of the distinguishing characteristics of family companies. When it comes to company operations, however, the border between family and firm may often blur, resulting in problems in transparency and fairness.

Financial transactions are a key example of this. Families must maintain the transparency of financial transactions, particularly those involving family members. This involves keeping detailed records of salary, dividends, and any other financial advantages given to family members. Transparency creates trust not just among family members but also among workers, stakeholders, and the larger society.

Decision-making is another crucial aspect. Major

decisions in many family enterprises are made informally at family gatherings or meals. However, it is critical to segregate family time from official business meetings for the purpose of fairness and ensuring that all perspectives are heard. Clear communication and ensuring that all family members, regardless of status in the family hierarchy, have a role in business decisions may help to reduce possible disputes.

### Guarding Legacy and Upholding Ethics

When one considers family companies, the concept of stewardship often comes to mind. Family members are caretakers of a heritage handed down through generations, not only corporate executives. While ensuring the business's continuity, this function requires an unwavering commitment to ethical issues.

Some of the world's most prominent family enterprises have historically encountered situations in which their duty as stewards was challenged against compelling financial imperatives. Consider the environmental issues that a family-owned mining firm can confront. While there is an immediate business benefit to ignoring environmental protections, the long-term consequences on the community and the company's image may be disastrous.

Furthermore, stewardship entails ensuring that the company does not become a platform for personal wealth at the cost of non-family workers or stakeholders. This includes assuring equitable remuneration, eliminating favoritism, and preventing commercial resources from being diverted to personal or family pursuits. While it may be tempting to support an event in which a family member is directly involved, the choice must be balanced against the true financial benefit that such a sponsorship would bring to the firm.

Ethical issues in family company management are inextricably tied to the concept of stewardship. It is about making decisions that respect the past while also benefiting the present and securing the future.

## Family Business Footprint: Shaping Communities & Societies

### Family Businesses as Pillars of Local Economies

Family businesses play an important role in developing local economies because of their strong roots in communities. Their influence, which may last decades, if not centuries, instills a degree of trust and reliance that modern companies cannot match.

Family enterprises are sometimes the major employers in smaller towns and cities. This empowers and obligates them to affect the economic health of these areas. Hiring local talent assures not just employment creation but also skill development within the community. Salary payments provide purchasing power for families, which encourages local companies and marketplaces. As these enterprises develop and expand over time, they indirectly support growth in auxiliary areas. For example, the development of a family-owned firm may result in the rise of logistics providers, local suppliers, and other service providers in the surrounding area (Reck et al., 2021).

Furthermore, these firms often support local events, festivals, and charities via sponsorships or by organizing them entirely. This not only develops a communal spirit but also encourages local tourism, which boosts the economy.

However, with power comes responsibility. Family business choices may have a large impact on the community. Decisions about downsizing or moving, for example, may have a considerable impact on local unemployment rates and economic health.

### How Family Business Narratives Shape Community Identities

In many parts of the globe, the tale of a small family company gets so embedded in the fabric of the town that it's difficult to separate the two. Through their operations, principles, and community activities, such enterprises end up shaping the very identity of the communities in which they operate.

Consider a fictitious town famed for its fine pottery, centered by a family firm that has mastered the technique for centuries. For both tourists and residents, the town's identity is inextricably linked to that family's past. The methods they offer, the designs they support, and the tales they tell become part of the collective narrative of the group.

Beyond the economic repercussions, family companies have a significant cultural and social effect. They often take on the role of stewards of local traditions and crafts, guaranteeing their preservation and spread. They help communities retain a feeling of pride and distinctiveness in an increasingly globalized world.

Furthermore, the values and ideals espoused by these firms often permeate the character of the neighborhood. If a family company sets a significant focus on sustainability, it is probable that the community will follow suit. In contrast, if a company disregards ethical issues, it may legitimize such conduct in the greater society.

## Strategies for maintaining a socially responsible business model

### Ensuring Ethical Operations

Family companies, which are frequently strongly anchored in their communities, emphasize the well-being of their stakeholders. They need a framework that smoothly connects commercial goals with a greater societal purpose to guarantee ethical operations. A transparent government is essential. It is critical to have clear ethical principles that govern corporate activities. This ethical mandate should support all aspects of the procurement, recruiting, and production operations.

Furthermore, regular stakeholder involvement has the potential to revolutionize. Interacting with workers, customers, suppliers, and even the wider community on a regular basis may provide insights into the business's socioeconomic influence. These encounters may indicate opportunities for improvement, ensuring that operations are in line with the needs and expectations of the community.

Another critical component is employee training. Ensuring that the staff knows and embraces the ethical mission may lead to increased consistency. Regular workshops and seminars concentrating on ethical issues unique to the business sector might aid in this attempt.

Maintaining an ethical business model, on the other hand, is not a one-time exercise. Internal and external audits, both internal and external, may assist in uncovering problem areas. These audits, if open and objective, may provide a path for continual development, ensuring that the company stays loyal to its ethical commitment throughout time.

**An Investment in the Future**

Sustainability is one of the most pressing issues of our day. This is particularly important for family companies, which often think in terms of generations. A sustainable company strategy tackles environmental issues while simultaneously ensuring long-term prosperity.

To begin, it is critical to understand the company's environmental impact. This entails examining activities to determine their environmental effect. Once recognized, these issues may be addressed by implementing greener technology, changing operating procedures, or even reinventing the company model itself.

Another emphasis is on supply chain sustainability. Ensuring that suppliers follow ecologically sound practices may enormously increase a company's beneficial effect. This might include favoring local suppliers, which minimizes transportation emissions, or collaborating with suppliers that have sustainability standards.

Innovativeproductdesignmayalsohelp.Designinggoods that use fewer resources, endure longer, or are biodegradable may help to decrease environmental damage dramatically. Furthermore, as customers grow more environmentally sensitive, these items might provide a business edge.

Engaging with stakeholders, particularly customers, may provide further insights. Their comments might lead to the creation of new, long-lasting goods or the improvement of current ones.

**A Long-Term Commitment for Family Businesses**

Transitioning to renewable energy sources is no longer an option in a society facing rising problems from climate change and resource depletion. With their long-term ambitions and commitments, family companies are particularly positioned to lead this shift.

Integrating renewable energy into company operations is fraught with difficulties. For example, the initial investment might be significant. Solar panels, wind turbines, and energy storage systems all demand large financial investments. However, the long-term advantages, both in terms of energy savings and a good influence on the environment, considerably surpass the initial expenses. Furthermore, governments all over the globe are increasingly providing incentives and subsidies to firms that invest in renewable energy, making the switch more financially feasible.

Then there's the issue of scalability. As the company expands, so does its energy use. To retain the advantages of the shift, it is critical that the renewable energy infrastructure grows with the company. This might include regular updates to the energy infrastructure or perhaps diversification into several renewable energy sources to maintain a steady supply.

Another factor to consider is community involvement. Family companies, which are often established in local communities, may leverage the shift to renewable energy to interact with these areas. Hosting renewable energy seminars, cooperating with local institutions on sustainability initiatives, and even granting community shares in renewable energy projects are all possible ways. Such programs not only improve the company's image but also instill a feeling of communal responsibility for the environment.

CHAPTER 11

# MANAGING FAMILY DYNAMICS

The intersection of personal connections and professional roles generates a complicated matrix in the intricate world of family enterprises. Family relations are at the center of this matrix, a powerful force that may either catapult a firm to new heights or become its Achilles' heel. Thus, skillfully controlling these dynamics is not only recommended but also required for the long-term success and peace of both the family and the company.

Emotions, history, and expectations all play a role in family relations. Past encounters, unsaid feelings, sibling rivalry, generational viewpoints, and ambitions weave a tapestry. When these dynamics enter the corporate world, they may have an impact on decision-making, strategic orientations, and day-to-day operations. For example, a previous personal quarrel between family members may impair their judgment in a business meeting, or generational differences may result in opposing opinions on corporate innovation.

Recognizing and resolving such dynamics is critical for a variety of reasons. For starters, unresolved family concerns might make it difficult to make clear and objective business judgments. Personal biases or emotions may cause what is beneficial for the company to be missed. This may limit development, innovation, and flexibility over time, making the company less competitive in its market.

Second, unresolved family dynamics may cause disputes that impede corporate operations. Power struggles, communication failures, and even legal problems may all result from such disagreements. Such interruptions not only have an immediate effect on business processes, but they may also taint the company's brand, undermining stakeholder confidence and consumer loyalty.

Furthermore, the well-being of family members is jeopardized. Personal relationships may be strained by ongoing conflicts and unsolved concerns, leading to alienation and suffering. Individual well-being might suffer as a result of the emotional toll, which can have an influence on their professional activities and contributions to the organization.

Positive family dynamics, on the other hand, based on trust, open communication, and mutual respect, maybe the foundation of a flourishing company. Families that successfully manage their dynamics capitalize on the power of long-standing connections, shared history, and mutual trust. This builds a strong foundation for the company, enabling it to weather problems, capitalize on opportunities, and leave a legacy that will last generations.

Managing family relations in family company management is equivalent to navigating the enterprise's own essence. It dives into the emotional and relational aspects that determine the direction of the company. By emphasizing this component, family enterprises may balance personal ties with professional demands, ensuring that the firm is not only lucrative but also a reflection of the family's values, unity, and vision.

## The role of family dynamics in business decisions

### Navigating Generational Shifts

Generational transfers in family businesses can result in a clash between tradition and modernization. Each generation brings its own set of experiences, values, and worldviews with it. The older generation may have developed the company on particular concepts and procedures that they believe are essential to the company's identity and success. In contrast, the younger generation may perceive newer, more efficient methods of doing things since they are exposed to a diverse socio-cultural and technical milieu.

This duality is fundamentally emotional as well as about changing business strategies. The oldest members may see the proposed changes as a disdain for their life's work, whilst the younger members may believe their potential is being suppressed. If such conflicts are not handled, they may have serious consequences for the firm, ranging from impeding innovation to causing shattered family relationships.

One method to deal with this is to encourage open communication. Regular family meetings in which each member is encouraged to voice their thoughts, regardless of age or position in the firm, may be quite beneficial. It is critical that the older generation understands that embracing new approaches does not always imply abandoning essential principles. Simultaneously, the younger members must approach change with caution, respecting the past's efforts and triumphs.

Another method is to clearly differentiate between family and business duties. It is necessary to define jobs based on skill rather than age or seniority. While the senior family member may be the CEO, a younger family member with a talent for digital marketing may be in charge of the company's internet initiatives. Such position definitions guarantee that the company benefits from the best of both worlds: expertise and innovation.

**Bridging Family Passion with Outside Expertise**

Incorporating outside expertise into a family company is sometimes regarded with skepticism. This opposition might be motivated by a variety of factors, including a desire to maintain family control, concerns about delegating key positions to outsiders, or just a desire to keep commercial affairs completely within the family. However, as family companies develop and the market advances, including outside knowledge, may become necessary to preserve competitiveness and stimulate innovation.

Family dynamics have an important influence on business decisions, influencing everything from firm strategy to day-to-day operational decisions. While anchored in years of history and shared experiences, these choices may often create echo chambers in which new ideas struggle to find a voice. External specialists who arrive without the baggage of family history but with a variety of experiences may contribute enormous value in this area.

Bringing in an outsider does more than simply bring in technical skills. They provide a new viewpoint, one unaffected by familial relationships. For example, although a family member may be hesitant to present a radical proposal for fear of upsetting senior relatives, an outside expert would be more impartial, based ideas only on commercial worth.

However, this integration is not without its difficulties. The challenge is to strike a balance between honoring the family's beliefs and empowering external specialists to effect genuine change. The importance of open communication cannot be overstated. Regular discussions in which family members and outside specialists offer their perspectives may aid in aligning everyone behind a single corporate objective.

## Advice on fostering open communication and trust

### Building Trust Outside the Boardroom

Taking a break from the daily grind of work may be a strong tool for fostering open communication and trust among family members. Retreats, whether official or informal, provide a unique opportunity for members to interact on a deeper level away from the demands of daily business choices. Away from the prying eyes of workers and stakeholders, the casual setting typically enables family members to express themselves more freely, enabling open communication.

Such getaways do not have to be pricey or elaborate. The fundamental purpose is to establish an atmosphere in which family members may express their problems, ambitions, and comments without fear of instant retribution. Structured activities, such as role-playing or team-building exercises, may be quite helpful in bridging communication gaps.

One of the most prevalent worries in family enterprises is the possibility of unresolved personal problems affecting professional choices. Retreats provide a chance to resolve underlying conflicts. Mediators or counselors might be engaged to guide talks, ensuring that they stay constructive and resolution-focused.

The true value of these retreats, however, resides in their potential to create mutual respect and understanding. Spending time together outside of the workplace allows family members to better understand each other's strengths and shortcomings. This greater knowledge may lead to a more harmonious working relationship in which trust is the cornerstone of every business decision.

**The Cornerstone of Constructive Communication**

The value of attentive listening cannot be emphasized in the world of family enterprises, where personal and professional borders sometimes blur. Understanding the feelings and intentions underlying the words is more important than just hearing what the other person is saying. Family members may overcome generational or experience gaps by practicing active listening and building a culture of mutual respect and trust.

Full concentration is required for active listening. In this day and age, it is critical for family members to be completely present during talks. This includes putting phones aside, avoiding side discussions, and maintaining eye contact. Nonverbal indications like these may go a long way toward making the speaker feel respected and heard.

Furthermore, active listening is refraining from making an initial judgment or formulating a response while the other person is still speaking. It's more about grasping the core of what's being stated. In order to guarantee that all parties are on the same page, ask open-ended questions, request clarifications, or simply paraphrase what has been stated.

Active listening may also be used to resolve conflicts in family companies where history and emotions run deep. It decreases the likelihood of misunderstandings and misinterpretations by ensuring that all parties feel heard. As family members practice and emphasize active listening, they create an atmosphere in which open communication flourishes and trust grows with each interaction.

**The Bedrock of Open Dialogue**

Establishing a culture that invites criticism might be the difference between stagnation and progress in the dynamic environment of a family company. When family members are encouraged to express their thoughts, concerns, and ideas without fear of repercussions, an ecology of continual development emerges.

When delivered constructively, feedback may be a tremendous tool for progress. It provides new insights, identifies opportunities for growth, and stimulates family members' engagement and ownership. However, in order for feedback to be useful, it must be provided and accepted in the proper spirit.

Setting clear criteria is the first step in creating a feedback-friendly culture. It is critical to define constructive feedback and distinguish it from simple criticism. Constructive feedback is problem-solving, detailed, and free of personal assaults. It is motivated by a desire to see the company flourish rather than by personal grudges.

Receiving comments gracefully is also essential. It entails accepting the input, meditating on its merits, and acting on it as necessary. Individuals who dismiss suggestions or get defensive may be discouraged from raising issues in the future.

Furthermore, frequent feedback meetings might be included in the company architecture. These established forums, whether monthly roundtable conversations or yearly retreats, may guarantee that feedback becomes an intrinsic part of the business's development plan.

# Boundaries & Battles: Navigating Conflict with Strategy

## Distinguishing Personal from Professional

Personal and professional divisions may sometimes blur in a family firm, resulting in circumstances where choices become emotionally charged rather than strategically thought out. Understanding the clear difference between these two domains is the core of a profitable family company. While family members share history, feelings, and relationships that bind them together, the commercial structure necessitates objective thinking free of sentimentality.

Creating a 'dual framework' might be a good place to start. This suggests that family members recognize and act in two different realms: one devoted to family dynamics and the other devoted solely to business. For example, business issues should not disturb family gatherings, and personal problems should not affect company choices.

Having precise job descriptions is one useful method. Each family member should have a clearly defined position in the firm, ensuring that they understand their obligations and the expectations that have been established for them. This reduces the possibility of overlapping responsibilities or treading on each other's toes, hence lowering possible disputes.

Regular family and work meetings, done separately, might also be useful. Family meetings may be about personal difficulties, goals, and events, but business meetings should be about the company's performance, strategy, and objectives.

Having a neutral facilitator or an external adviser present during these sessions may help give a balanced viewpoint and keep talks on course.

The dual framework requires both conceptual and structural adjustments. It underlines the significance of considering the company as a distinct entity with its own set of rules, expectations, and results.

**The Art of Negotiated Consensus**

Conflict resolution is an inherent difficulty in any organization, but it is especially difficult in family enterprises owing to the deep interweaving of personal connections and professional positions. Conflicts, rather than being seen negatively, may be viewed as chances for progress if treated with maturity and a systematic resolution framework.

First and foremost, accepting that disagreements may emerge is half the fight fought. After that, the emphasis should move to fostering an atmosphere favorable to open conversation. Transparency is essential. Encouraging members to express their concerns without fear of being judged or retaliated against may pave the path for open and honest dialogues.

Active listening is quite important. Conflicts often worsen because the people involved feel unheard. Many misconceptions may be avoided by ensuring that each person has a chance to share their point of view and that others really listen.

Once all points of view have been presented, the next stage is to locate common ground. It is important to recognize that consensus does not always imply total agreement. Instead, it represents a group decision that all participants can embrace, even if it was not their first option.

It may be advantageous to employ an external mediator in cases when disagreements are deeply established or achieving a consensus seems difficult. A neutral third person may give an impartial viewpoint, assisting family members in navigating the disagreement and reaching a resolution.

### The Use of Third-Party Mediators in Diffusing Family Business Tensions

Conflicts in family enterprises may sometimes grow to the point where internal settlement becomes difficult. A third-party mediator may be quite helpful in this situation. A third-party mediator, unlike family members, does not have emotional connections or a history with the family, enabling them to approach issues objectively.

A prevalent misunderstanding is that seeking external mediation indicates a failure or incapacity to handle internal matters. On the contrary, it demonstrates maturity and a real willingness to address challenges for the benefit of the company. Professional mediators are educated to manage complicated human dynamics while maintaining a primary emphasis on the success of the company.

In cases when family members have entrenched viewpoints, the mediator may assist in bridging communication barriers. They guarantee that each participant feels heard and understood by promoting organized discourse. They may also bring fresh ideas or solutions to the table that family members may not have considered.

Mediators may also help to build long-term dispute resolution systems. They may offer tactics or structures, such as a family council or frequent family business meetings, to resolve possible problems based on the dynamics of the family and the nature of the company.

The presence of an outside mediator might serve as a reminder that the survival and development of the firm are vital. Personal differences are unavoidable, but they should never threaten the company's heritage or future possibilities. Family companies that seek mediation demonstrate their commitment to continuity, expansion, and shared success.

CHAPTER 12

# GLOBAL AND CULTURAL PERSPECTIVES

With the advent of globalization, the landscape of family companies, which has historically been based in local communities and cultures, has undergone seismic upheavals. Many family companies now operate in or are impacted by, a worldwide economy, making global and cultural views critical. Engaging with different viewpoints is not a choice; it is a need for family companies seeking to prosper in today's linked world.

The awareness that various cultures have varied perspectives on family and business and the complicated connection between the two is at the heart of this discussion. A strong understanding of these cultural differences is essential for a family company wishing to grow internationally or work with foreign partners. In one culture, a business activity that is considered typical may be seen as unprofessional or even insulting in another. As a result, comprehending and adjusting to these subtleties might be the difference between a successful endeavor and a diplomatic gaffe.

Furthermore, global views expose family firms to a plethora of operational approaches, managerial styles, and creative initiatives used by family businesses throughout the globe. Such exposure may be a goldmine of information, enabling organizations to absorb best practices from across the world, fine-tune their operations, and gain a competitive advantage.

Furthermore, global and cultural viewpoints are critical in extending the client base. Understanding the interests, attitudes, and purchasing patterns of various client categories becomes more important when family companies expand into worldwide markets. This influences not just product or service changes but also marketing tactics, communication methods, and interaction platforms.

On the other hand, family enterprises offer their own cultural diversity to the world stage. They may use their lineage, customs, and family values as distinctive selling advantages, providing a particular flavor in a global market that is becoming more homogenized. This might result in the creation of specialized markets or devoted client groups that respect the authenticity and legacy that family enterprises radiate.

Engaging with global viewpoints also prepares family enterprises for cross-border difficulties. A global vision provides family companies with the foresight to foresee and manage issues, whether it's managing foreign legislation, recognizing global economic trends, or minimizing risks connected with geopolitical upheavals.

The fabric of family company management is enriched by global and cultural viewpoints. They extend the view by integrating various thoughts, processes, and possibilities into the organization. These perspectives are the lenses through which family businesses can envision and actualize their growth, ensuring they remain relevant, competitive, and influential on the global stage in an era where boundaries are increasingly blurred, markets are interconnected, and businesses are part of a global ecosystem.

## Overview of family businesses around the world

**Traditions Meets Modernization**

Asia has been a hotspot for family enterprises due to its complex tapestry of cultures, customs, and economic dynamism. Family firms in India, China, South Korea, and Japan have not only dominated their domestic markets but also had a worldwide impact.

Historically, Confucian ideals in China and comparable traditional values in adjacent nations stressed respect for elders, familial loyalty, and a feeling of responsibility for one's heritage. This has frequently translated into a patriarchal system in which business leadership is passed down from father to eldest son. Similarly, in India, the joint family structure was important in how enterprises were handled, with decisions being made collaboratively, valuing agreement over individual ambition.

Globalization and the quick rate of technological improvements, on the other hand, have ushered in a wave of modernity. Younger generations, who have been educated abroad and exposed to many business approaches, are returning with a wider viewpoint. While they value traditions, they also acknowledge the importance of innovation and global competitiveness. This clash of history and modernity may create conflicts since heritage traditions do not necessarily fit with the new corporate strategy.

Nonetheless, the fusion of these two realms has resulted in extraordinary success stories. A family business's adaptability and personal touch, paired with worldwide best practices, maybe a powerful combination. Many Asian family firms, for example, are increasingly concentrating on sustainable practices, digital transformation, and diversification into new areas, all while maintaining basic family values.

**Latin American Family Businesses:**

Family companies have a long history in Latin America and continue to be an important foundation of the region's economy. Brazil, Mexico, Argentina, and Chile all have family companies that range from agriculture to industry to services.

The durability of Latin American family companies is one of its distinguishing features. The area has suffered several economic issues throughout the years, ranging from hyperinflation to debt crises. Nonetheless, many family companies have successfully navigated these tumultuous seas by combining flexibility, strong community links, and a profound sense of purpose.

Latin America has a strong importance on family and community, and this extends to the corporate world. Decision-making is inclusive, with seniors consulted, but a real effort is made to engage and understand the perspectives of younger people. This mix of expertise and innovation has been critical to the long-term viability of many firms.

However, Latin American family enterprises, like those in other areas, encounter obstacles. As firms develop and expand, there is an increasing demand to professionalize operations, which may often conflict with conventional business practices. Nonetheless, many organizations are becoming aware of this and are actively attempting to establish a balance between professional management and family values.

The rising importance of women in leadership positions in family enterprises has been a noticeable development in the area. While leadership has historically been male-dominated, there is a rising recognition of the qualities and views that women bring to the table. This trend is not only affecting economic relationships, but it is also impacting larger society perspectives.

## Regional Nuances in Family Business Management

Europe, with its different cultures, languages, and history, makes for an intriguing study of the impact of cultural influences on family business management. On the surface, European family companies seem to have a lot in common. However, if one digs a bit further, specific geographical traits that affect business attitudes might be discovered.

Family companies in Mediterranean countries such as Italy and Spain generally represent close-knit family structures. The value of loyalty, respect for elders, and protecting the family name cannot be overstated. This often translates into a corporate strategy that stresses long-term stability above short-term profits. Relationships are important, and many agreements are closed based on mutual trust built over years, if not decades.

Professionalism and structure are more valued in northern nations such as Germany and Sweden. Family enterprises in these areas may be able to more clearly segregate family problems from business talks. It is fairly commonplace for family members to get experience outside of the family company before being given a key job inside it.

The United Kingdom adds another hue to this vibrant tapestry. Because of their colonial heritage and worldwide ties, many British family firms have a more global vision. While family values are still important, there is often a strong feeling of adapting to global best practices.

In all of these nations, the cultural fabric has a significant impact on family business decision-making, succession planning, and dispute resolution. Recognizing these distinctions is critical for anybody interested in engaging with or understanding the dynamics of European family companies.

**African Family Enterprises:**

In the context of family enterprises, Africa, frequently referred to as the birthplace of humanity, provides a dynamic interaction between age-old traditions and the winds of change. The continent, with over fifty nations and a diverse range of races and languages, provides significant insights into the impact of culture in building family business ethics.

The notion of 'family' goes beyond the nuclear unit in many African traditions, covering extended relatives and sometimes whole towns. This wide concept is often used in corporate activities. An African family business may involve not just close family members but also distant relatives and community members. This inclusiveness may result in a strong support system, but it can also present issues in terms of job clarity and decision-making structures.

Many African companies have traditionally been based on agriculture and commerce. With the family serving as the major unit of labor and resource allocation, decisions were often taken jointly, with the well-being of the whole group in mind. However, as urbanization grows and industries expand, there is a shift toward more organized and formal corporate procedures.

Even if new management approaches are used, a strong undercurrent of old values remains. Respect for elders, the value of compromise, and faith in the common good are strongly ingrained. These values may occasionally collide with current business imperatives, but they can also be used to establish a distinct, value-driven corporate strategy.

## Global Management: Strategies Across Cultures

### The Dichotomy of Family Business Management in Asia and Europe

The comparison of Asian and European family enterprises provides fascinating insights into how various cultures approach management. Asian family businesses, particularly those in China, India, and Japan, are steeped in tradition. In China, Confucian ideals stress hierarchy, loyalty, and reverence for elders, resulting in a top-down management system. Decisions are often centralized, with the patriarch or matriarch exerting significant control. The emphasis is often on long-term development, and succession is generally based on bloodline, with the oldest son being favored.

In contrast, European family firms, notably in Germany, France, and the United Kingdom, have shifted to a more democratic and professional management approach. While tradition is still respected, there is a greater focus on meritocracy. Succession planning is on capacity more than lineage. Many European family firms urge their children to obtain experience outside of the family company before taking on key positions.

It is important to highlight, however, that globalization is blurring fundamental boundaries. Asian family firms are rapidly embracing Western management principles, placing a premium on professionalism, corporate governance, and diversification. In contrast, European corporations respect the close-knit family relationships and long-term vision observed in their Asian counterparts. However, each region's underlying cultural mindset guarantees that the essential element of family company management stays different.

**From the Sands of Arabia to the Highlands of South America:**

Emerging economies provide a diverse range of family company management methods, each inspired by its own combination of history, culture, and modernity. Family businesses are an important part of the Middle Eastern economy. These enterprises, which are rooted in Bedouin trading and hospitality traditions, place a premium on respect, reputation, and family history. Management is often patriarchal, and corporate operations are inextricably linked to personal connections. In the Arab business sector, where a person's word is frequently shared, networking and trust are critical.

Compare this to South American family enterprises, particularly in Brazil, Argentina, and Chile. The impact of Spanish and Portuguese colonial history meets indigenous traditions here. This region's family enterprises exhibit a strong and occasionally turbulent blend of emotion and practicality. While familial connections are strong, the region's economic instability has forced some flexibility and adaptation in management tactics. Businesses must often be nimble in order to react to the ebb and flow of economic tides.

The problem of industrialization and globalization, however, is a similar thread in both places. As family companies attempt to grow outside their boundaries, they face the challenge of incorporating global best practices while retaining their own cultural character. The dance between tradition and modernity is a delicate one, requiring finesse and strategic foresight.

### African and North American Family Business Paradigms

The African and North American continents, each unique in their own way, provide intriguing stories of how family enterprises have grown and adapted to their unique difficulties and possibilities.

Family companies, ranging from small-scale firms to massive conglomerates, are an important component of the African economy. African family companies are profoundly community-oriented, influenced by tribal ties, community relationships, and a complex tapestry of traditions. Their management techniques often favor community benefit over pure profit, assessing economic performance in terms of greater societal influence. Succession in these companies may not just be familial; it may also extend to persons beyond the immediate family but within the larger community, depending on trust and capacity. Economic constraints, political insecurity in certain parts, and the urgent need for modernization have resulted in a hybrid of classic and creative business techniques to assure company continuity and development.

On the other hand, North America, which includes the United States and Canada, represents a landscape in which family companies have gone through numerous stages of development. Influenced by waves of immigration, industrialization, and technological breakthroughs, family companies in the region have evolved from modest mom-and-pop shops in the early twentieth century to varied firms spanning many industries by the twenty-first century. They face challenges such as intense competition, maintaining family cohesion in an individualistic society, and navigating the complexities of wealth management and inheritance despite having access to sophisticated management tools, professionalization, and a structured approach to succession.

Despite these geographical disparities, both continents demonstrate family companies' flexibility and durability. Whether it's via the application of ancient knowledge, the adoption of contemporary management methods, or a combination of the two, family companies in Africa and North America highlight the universal reality that, at the core of such organizations, it's always about reconciling family values with corporate values.

# CONCLUSION

In digging into the area of "Family Business Management," we have traveled through the complex tapestry of what helps family companies not just survive but flourish in the face of a plethora of difficulties and possibilities. As we near the end of our journey, it becomes critical to capture the deep insights and information gained, providing a compass for those who embark on or continue to navigate the seas of family businesses.

The essence of a family company, as defined, lies not only in its definition but also in the ubiquity of such businesses throughout sectors and industries. Their pervasiveness, punctuated by different traits, creates obstacles, which are often exacerbated by the merging of family emotions and commercial choices. It's a dance between the emotions and the head, between personal relationships and professional objectives.

Our in-depth examination of ownership and governance revealed the several methods that family firms may use. The need to achieve a balance between family ambitions and work goals became clear. Governance isn't just about leading; it's about leading with a grasp of familial intricacies, ensuring that the family's fabric stays intact even as the firm moves forward.

One of the most powerful thoughts has been on succession planning. The survival of family enterprises, which typically span decades, is dependent on rigorous planning. It's not only about selecting a successor but also about preparing them, ensuring that the company's culture and family values remain its guiding lights.

When personal and professional lives collide, disagreements are unavoidable. However, as we've seen, it's not the disputes themselves that characterize the success of family enterprises but how they're resolved. The necessity of communication, understanding, and sometimes even compromise in guaranteeing the enterprise's survival and health cannot be understated.

Another component emerged: financial management, with family companies requiring savvy financial strategies not just for survival but also for expansion. Intergenerational wealth management and protecting the company's financial future became obvious priorities.

The human factor, both inside the family and among the staff, added to the complications. Family companies, as recognized, need a distinct strategy for recruiting, training, and developing people while also ensuring that the work culture reflects family values.

With the globe in perpetual motion, corporate development and innovation have emerged as key issues. The need to adapt to change and ensure that the firm stays relevant in changing times was emphasized.

However, any voyage, no matter how profitable, may eventually come to an end or a new beginning. The exit alternatives mentioned provided a framework for how family company leaders may transition, whether handing the mantle to the next generation or making the difficult choice to sell.

Navigating legal problems and maintaining tax compliance emerged as critical, not just from a regulatory standpoint, but also to safeguard the company and its history.

The case studies offered both inspiration and insights by drawing on the experiences of others. These richly experienced anecdotes highlighted the opportunities, obstacles, and routes to success in the family business environment.

The ethical and social obligation assumed by family enterprises has been a constant subject and probably one of the most significant. Their influence on society and communities, not simply the market, makes them vital.

Personal complexities, dynamics, emotions, and connections all played a role in understanding family enterprises. Managing these relations, developing trust, and establishing limits emerged as difficulties as well as answers.

While family companies may be specific, their essence, problems, and accomplishments are universal, as shown by our worldwide review. Cultural subtleties, regional customs, and global plans all came together to portray a vision of family companies as global organizations with localized souls.

# REFERENCES


*Governing the Family-Run Business.* (2001, September 4). HBS Working Knowledge. https://hbswk.hbs.edu/item/governing-the-family-run-business

Gillis, A. S., Daniel, D., & Snider, E. (2021, November 17). *succession planning.* HR Software. https://www.techtarget.com/searchhrsoftware/definition/succession-planning#:~:text=Succession%20planning%20is%20a%20process,not%2Dfor%2Dprofit%20sectors.

Kenton, W. (2022, November 29). *Succession Planning Basics: How It Works, Why It's Important.* Investopedia. https://www.investopedia.com/terms/s/succession-planning.asp

*Managing conflict in a family-owned business.* (n.d.). Baker Tilly. https://www.bakertilly.com/insights/managing-conflict-in-a-family-owned-business#:~:text=Communicate%20openly%20and%20honestly%3A%20As,what%20others%20have%20to%20say.

Bautista, R. (2018, March 20). *5 Steps to Overcome Conflicts in Family Business | Business Management.* INSIGHTS: The Guthrie-Jensen Blog. https://guthriejensen.com/blog/5-steps-to-overcome-conflicts-in-family-business/

P. (2020, October 30). *Financial management and family businesses*. Nexa. https://www.nexa.law/financial-management-and-family-businesses/

*Human Resources in Family Business: Maximizing the Power of Your People - The Family Business Consulting Group*. (2021, June 24). The Family Business Consulting Group. https://www.thefbcg.com/resource/human-resources-in-family-business/

*Human Resources is a Vital Part of Any Family Business*. (n.d.). https://www.familybusinessmagazine.com/human-resources-critical-part-effective-family-business

*Your business: Growth and innovation*. (n.d.). https://www.ey.com/en_uk/family-business/growth-innovation

*Innovation in Family Business - The Family Business Consulting Group*. (2020, July 1). The Family Business Consulting Group. https://www.thefbcg.com/resource/innovation-in-family-business/

Garcia, S. (2023, March 1). *Effective Exit Strategies for Family Businesses*. www.bizbuysell.com. https://www.bizbuysell.com/learning-center/article/exit-strategies-family-business/

*Succession planning: 4 exit strategies when leaving the family business*. (2023, May 4). BDC.ca. https://www.bdc.ca/en/articles-tools/change-ownership/plan-succession/family-succession-4-common-exit-strategies

K. (2023, August 8). *Tax Considerations for Family Businesses*.

Ridgefield Consulting. https://www.ridgefieldconsulting.co.uk/tax-guides/tax-benefits-for-family-businesses/

Peek, S. (2023, April 10). *Taking Advantage of Tax Deductions For Your Home Business*. https://www.uschamber.com/co/. https://www.uschamber.com/co/run/finance/home-based-business-tax-deductions

*Strategy Study: How Walmart Became The Retailer Of The People*. (n.d.). https://www.cascade.app/studies/walmart-strategy-study

Reck, F. S., Fischer, D., & Brettel, M. (2021, March 8). *Ethical Decision-Making in Family Firms: The Role of Employee Identification*. Journal of Business Ethics; Springer Science+Business Media. https://doi.org/10.1007/s10551-021-04774-8

*The Study of the Relations among Ethical Considerations, Family Management and Organizational Performance in Corporate Governance on JSTOR*. (n.d.). https://www.jstor.org/stable/25123905

*Six Tips for Managing Family Dynamics*. (2020, July 14). Giving Compass. https://givingcompass.org/partners/ncfp-magazine/six-tips-managing-family-dynamics

*Managing Family Dynamics :: Leeza's Care Connection*. (n.d.). https://leezascareconnection.org/home/resources/im-new-caregiving-now-what-2/family-dynamics

# ABOUT AUTHOR

Dr. Andreas Svoboda stands as a distinguished figure in the spheres of finance, insurance, and academia. Presently, he holds esteemed positions as a Professor at the United International Business Schools in Zurich, and as the Head of Finance and Leadership, Banking and Finance at the Swiss Distance University of Applied Sciences (FFHS). Beyond his academic roles, Dr. Andreas Svoboda is the visionary behind THE Insurance Academy and Vision Goal LLC, showcasing his keen entrepreneurial flair.

With an illustrious career in finance, he possesses advanced qualifications such as an LL.M. in International Business Law and a Doctor of Business Administration. His proficiency is further accentuated by his multilingual capabilities, diverse publications, and prominent certifications including the Certified Financial Planner (CFP®). Through 'Svoboda Finance' on YouTube, Dr. Andreas Svoboda extends his wealth of knowledge, illuminating the path to financial literacy for many.

Milton Keynes UK
Ingram Content Group UK Ltd.
UKHW040716201123
432908UK00002B/437